WHAT

GOES

ON

Poetry

Everything Else in the World
The Insistence of Beauty
Local Visitations
Different Hours
Loosestrife
New and Selected Poems, 1974–1994
Landscape at the End of the Century
Between Angels
Local Time
Not Dancing
Work and Love
A Circus of Needs
Full of Lust and Good Usage
Looking for Holes in the Ceiling

Prose

Walking Light: Essays and Memoirs
Riffs & Reciprocities

Chapbooks

Five Impersonations
Winter at the Caspian Sea (with Lawrence Raab)

WHAT

GOES

ON

SELECTED & NEW POEMS

1995–2009

STEPHEN DUNN

W. W. NORTON & COMPANY

NEW YORK | LONDON

For information about permission to reproduce selections from
this book, write to Permissions, W. W. Norton & Company, Inc.,
500 Fifth Avenue, New York, NY 10110

For information about special discounts for bulk purchases,
please contact W. W. Norton Special Sales at
specialsales@wwnorton.com or 800-233-4830

Manufacturing by Courier Westford
Book design by JAM Design
Production manager: Devon Zahn

Library of Congress Cataloging-in-Publication Data

Dunn, Stephen, date.
What goes on : selected & new poems 1995–2009 / Stephen Dunn. — 1st
ed.
p. cm.
Includes index.
ISBN 978-0-393-06775-0 (hardcover)
I. Title.
PS3554.U49W47 2008
813'.54—dc22

2008028062

W. W. Norton & Company, Inc.
500 Fifth Avenue, New York, N.Y. 10110
www.wwnorton.com

W. W. Norton & Company Ltd.
Castle House, 75/76 Wells Street, London W1T 3QT

1 2 3 4 5 6 7 8 9 0

for

BARBARA

CONTENTS

from LOCAL VISITATIONS (2003)

from THE INSISTENCE OF BEAUTY (2004)

from EVERYTHING ELSE IN THE WORLD (2006)

NEW POEMS

Men and women sleep not with each other but with the memories, the regrets, the hopes of unions yet to come. Our adulteries are internal; they deepen our aloneness.

—GEORGE STEINER

But then life always makes you choose between two possibilities, and you always feel: One is missing! Always one—the uninvented third possibility.

—ROBERT MUSIL

Only the hidden god is the true god, for the god who can be known has already become an artifact of conscious culture, and is in the process of disappearing.

—JAMES HOLLIS

from

LOOSESTRIFE

(1996)

TUCSON

A man was dancing with the wrong woman
in the wrong bar, the wrong part of town.
He must have chosen the woman, the place,
as keenly as you choose what to wear
when you dress to kill.
And the woman, who could have said no,
must have made her choice years ago,
to look like the kind of trouble
certain men choose as their own.
I was there for no good reason myself,
with a friend looking for a friend,
but I'm not important.
They were dancing close
when a man from the bar decided
the dancing was wrong. I'd forgotten
how fragile the face is, how fists too
are just so many small bones.
The bouncer waited, then broke in.
Someone wiped up the blood.
The woman began to dance
with another woman, each in tight jeans.
The air pulsed. My hands
were fidgety, damp.
We were Mexicans, Indians, whites.
The woman was part this, part that.
My friend said nothing's wrong, stay put,
it's a good fighting bar, you won't get hurt
unless you need to get hurt.

WILD

The year I owned a motorcycle and split the air
in southern Spain, and could smell the oranges
in the orange groves as I passed them
outside of Seville, I understood
I'd been riding too long in cars,
probably even should get a horse,
become a high-up, flesh-connected thing
among the bulls and cows.
My brand-new wife had a spirit
that worried and excited me, a history
of moving on. Wine from a spigot for pennies,
langostinas and angulas, even the language
felt dangerous in my mouth. Mornings,
our icebox bereft of ice,
I'd speed on my motorcycle to the iceman's house,
strap a big rectangular block
to the extended seat where my wife often sat
hot behind me, arms around my waist.
In the streets the smell of olive oil,
the noise of men torn between church
and sex, their bodies taut, heretical.
And the women, buttoned-up,
or careless, full of public joy, a Jesus
around their necks.
Our neighbors showed us how to shut down
in the afternoon,
the stupidity of not respecting the sun.
They forgave us who we were.
Evenings we'd take turns with the *Herald Tribune*
killing mosquitoes, our bedroom walls bloody
in this country known for blood;
we couldn't kill enough.
When the Levante, the big wind, came out of Africa

with its sand and heat, disturbing things,
it brought with it a lesson, unlearnable,
of how far a certain wildness can go.
Our money ran out. I sold the motorcycle.
We moved without knowing it
to take our quieter places in the world.

ARS POETICA

I'd come to understand restraint
is worthless unless
something's about to spill or burst,

and that the Commandments
understand us perfectly, a large No
for the desirability of everything

vengeful, delicious, out of reach.
I wanted to write ten things
that contained as much.

Maybe from the beginning
the issue was how to live
in a world so extravagant

it had a sky,
in bodies so breakable
we had to pray.

I welcomed, though,
our celestial freedom, our promiscuous flights
all returning to earth.

Yet what could awe us now?
The feeling dies
and then the word.

Restraint. Extravagance. I liked
how one could unshackle the other,
that they might become indivisible.

Astaire's restraint was a kind of extravagance,
while Ginger Rogers danced backwards
in high heels and continued to smile!

She had such grace it was unfair
we couldn't keep our eyes off him,
but the beautiful is always unfair.

I found myself imagining him
gone wild, gyrating, leaping,
his life suddenly uncontainable.

Oh, even as he thrashed,
I could tell he was feeling
for limits, and what he could bear.

THE SONG

Late at night a song
breaks off, unfinished,
that rose from the street
outside your apartment,
not a cry but a song,
and something you recognize
as sadness
comes over you.
The street is empty
when you look.
The sadness, too,
is not locatable,
a referent lost somewhere
like an address book
from one of your other lives
with a page missing,
names that must
have mattered once.
A woman was singing
or perhaps a man
with the kind of voice
that has so much woman in it
you should fear for his safety.
The song was familiar,
and it strikes you now
that maybe you were dreaming
or even, yes, it was you
yourself singing.
All night you wait
for it to start again.
There's only the sound
of cars, and, nearer,
though you can't get that near,

your heart.
You've faked so many feelings
in your time you wonder
if it could have been
the ghost of faked feelings
offering you an authentic sadness,
a gift. But you're so tired,
so on that edge
between clarity and silliness,
you might think anything.
Dawn comes with its intermittency,
its tempo that hasn't
yet lengthened into traffic.
You haven't slept, you swear it,
though you know
when it comes to that
most people are mistaken.

IMAGINING MYSELF MY FATHER

I drove slowly, the windows open,
letting the emptiness within meet
the brotherly emptiness without.
Deer grazed the Parkway's edge,
solemnly enjoying their ridiculous,
gentle lives. There were early signs
of serious fog.

Salesman with a product
I had to pump myself up to sell,
merchant of my own hope,
friend to every tollbooth man,
I named the trees I passed.
I knew the dwarf pines,
and why in such soil
they could grow only so tall.

A groundhog wobbled from the woods.
It, too, seemed ridiculous,
and I conjured for it a wild heart,
at least a wild heart.
My dashboard was agleam with numbers
and time.

It was the kind of morning
the dark never left.
The truly wild were curled up, asleep,
or in some high nest looking down.
There was no way they'd let us love them
just right.

I said "fine" to those who asked.
I told them about my sons, athletes both.
All day I moved among men
who claimed they needed nothing,
nothing, at least, that I had.
Maybe another time, they said.
Or, Sorry, things are slow.

On the drive back
I drove fast, and met the regulars
at the Inn for a drink.
It seemed to me a man needed a heart
for the road, and a heart for home,
and one more for his friends.

And so many different, agile tongues.

GRACE

After the 1993 World Series

Mulholland extended his hand to Williams,
eased him away from the polite avidity
of reporters—good men mostly,
just doing their jackal job for us.

Didn't we want to know exactly
what public failure felt like?
Mulholland extended his hand
because he couldn't bear what had gone

several questions too long, and Williams,
the wild thing, answering them all straight
down the middle. Mulholland must have known
but for some grace . . . some luck . . .

and how a public man is always a mistake
or two from ruin.
He extended his hand to Williams
while the rest of us watched from our safe

carpeted dens, and the Toronto players
celebrated properly in their locker room.
Back in Jersey, vandals already had thrown eggs
at Williams's house, young men no doubt

without doubt who felt others should die
for them and succeed for them and make them
happy. Oh the luxury of failing in private!
Mulholland extended his hand to Williams

who took it and walked out
of the camera's exacting eye, and into history.
Other teammates, sad themselves,
tried to console him, unsure just then—

as we were—if sympathy could reach
all the hard way to forgiveness.

CRIMINAL

After Tonya & Nancy

One woman has nothing out of place
as she slides into our living rooms.
The other can't control her face,

the past is in it, and something cheap insists
on the wrong, expensive gowns.
Unnerving, though: nothing out of place.

We know no one is quite that chaste;
always near the palace are the ruins.
The other can't control her face,

yet it's so hard for us to embrace
her, even broken-laced and fallen.
One woman has nothing out of place

and, more unfair, she's all art and excellence.
Turn away, egalitarians.
The other who never learned to control her face

applauds politely, smiles; what grace
she's willed lasts only seconds.
One is beautiful, has nothing out of place.
The other can't control her face.

TIGER FACE

Because you can be what you're not
   for only so long,
one day the tiger cub raised by goats

wandered to the lake and saw himself.
   It was astounding
to have a face like that, cat-handsome,

hornless, and we can imagine he stared
   a long time, then sipped
and pivoted, bemused yet burdened now

with choice. The mother goat had nursed him.
   The others had tolerated
his silly quickness and claws.

And because once you know who you are
   you need not rush,
and good parents are a blessing

whoever they are, he went back to them,
   rubbing up against
their bony shins, keeping his secret to himself.

But after a while the tiger who'd found
   his true face
felt the disturbing hungers, those desires

to get low in the reeds, swish his tail,
   charge.
Because he was a cat he disappeared

without goodbyes, his goat-parents relieved
  such a thing was gone.
And we can imagine how, alone and beyond

choice, he wholly became who he was—
  that zebra or gazelle
stirring the great blood rush and odd calm

as he discovered, while moving, what needed
  to be done.

THE LIVING

Our trees limb-heavy and silver—
the beautiful never more on the edge
of breaking—and the indiscriminate
freezing rain slicking
the side streets and back alleys,
the long driveways of the rich.

Nothing moving except kids, the stopped world
just slippery to them, permissive, good.

Our cupboards are near empty.
The liquor cabinet, too.
Under the eaves unfrozen logs
in case the electricity goes.
Bosnians, Sudanese, flicker into our lives,
flicker out. To think of them is to lose
any right to complain.

Will the mail get through? What is uppermost
and most deep down?
I'd like to feel, once again, what I know.

Now a lone car, braving it, going slow,
kids on its fender.
Icicles exclamatory from the shed's roof.
What's underneath is sure
to have something underneath it.
All the way in: that's where crazy is.
The cable's out, or down.
The TV screen is snow.

A branch snaps,
and the comparisons that come
are whipcrack, gunshot—the almost dead.
What to do with the barely living
before they die? Exhaust them, I say,
shellac them with our tongues.
Isn't overuse a form of love?
Like a gunshot; like a whipcrack; both,
one last time.

The forecast is more of the same.
And then a few things worse.

I feel like making a little path
from house to car,
then I'm going to scrape.
Wait until it all stops, my wife says.
Is she a realist or an optimist?
I've got my coat on.
I've got the hard-edged shovel in my hand.

THE REFUGE

The snow geese took off in fours,
sometimes in fives, while the great blue heron,
singular and majestically weird,
complicated a rivulet. An egret,
fishing, did its lascivious Groucho Marx
walk, only slowly, neck and head
in odd accord, and hundreds of black ducks,
driven by memory, readied themselves
in the curious calm of New Jersey
for that long flight beyond winter.
        This was the safe place,
famous for these birds and meetings
of adulterous lovers, everything endangered
protected. Turtle Cove was closed
to humans; the dunlin and the swan
acted as if the world weren't harsh, maniacal.
Absecon Bay stretched out toward the Atlantic,
the very ocean Burt Lancaster said—
with the wild accuracy of a saddened heart—
wasn't the same anymore. The horizon graphed
the ziggy, unequal stretch of casino hotels,
and in front of us on the hard, dirt road
gulls dropped clam shells from a height
so perfect they opened.
        I had come with my sister-in-law,
nephew and niece, a familial gesture, not exactly
my style. My brother was back on the couch
watching football, my wife cooking
the Thanksgiving dinner that soon would bring us
together. Which one of us didn't need
to be thanked, and eventually forgiven?
A herring gull swallowed an eel.
Walking, the great blue heron

lost all of its grandeur. In a few hours
my brother would say grace at the table,
and we'd bow our heads, almost seriously,
but for now it was red-winged blackbird
and Canada goose, it was marshland and sky,
all the easily praised, the nothing like us.

LOOSESTRIFE

1

Storms moved across the Rockies
and through the plains, rode the jet stream
east. By the time they reached us: rain.
And there were other things that looked—
to other eyes—like welcome news.
The country tilting right.
A few more punishments for the poor.
It was the winter winter never came
to South Jersey; no natural equivalent,
once again, to our lives. All around us
a harshness, a severity, not destined soon
to stop. Oh we were part of it,
reserved ourselves for just a few,
held back instead of gave. Our hearts:
caged things, no longer beating
for the many, who were too many now.
Meanwhile, the Dakotas were snowed in.
A bad wind came off the lakes,
and Chicago and Buffalo braced
for a familiar misery, predictable,
the satisfaction, at least, of what was due.
Here the sun came out and stayed for days.
It wasn't cold enough to think of warmth.
For months, it seemed, we lived lower
in the nation, seasonless, the answers
mostly Christian, though far from Christlike,
to every hard and bitter question.

2

The impatient, upstart crocuses
and daffodils fell once again
for the lies of March.
They simply wanted to exist.
The warm sun must have said Now,
and they gave themselves
to that first, hardly refusable touch.
History was whispering
at least another frost,
but who listens to the hushed sobrieties
of the old? The daffodils died
the advantaged death
of those with other deaths to live.
We stripped down, got colds.
Heraclitus, I want to say I've stepped
into the same stream twice,
and everything felt the same.
It wasn't, I know that now,
but what it felt like
had a truth of its own.
The daffodils and crocuses
traveled through the solitude
of what they felt
toward what they might become.
Choiceless, reactive, inhuman—
nothing to admire in what they did.

3

A superior sky mottled in the west,
the water beneath it glassy, still.
As I crossed the bridge, there it was:
the landscape's invitation to forget.
An osprey swooped low, disreputable
as birds go, but precise, efficient,
a banker in wing-tips, office-bound,
ready to foreclose.
We live in a postcard, I thought,
cropped, agreeably, to deceive;
beyond its edges
broken glass at the schoolyard,
routine boredom, decency, spite.
And then the white, wood-framed
colonials on either side of 575,
Sinton's apple orchard, the shack
with three old cars in front of it,
its porch slanted, no one ever home.
The mowed field and the field wild
with rockrose and goat's rue
declared themselves as property, ours,
no one else's, and I acknowledged
how good the differentiating spaces were
between people and people,
I, who, years ago—
acolyte to an era's pious clarities—
went home to accuse
my dear parents of being capitalists.

4

Clear nights I looked upward and said,
"My God," a figure of speech,
another exhalation of surprise.
The sky was enormous, a planetarium
without walls, the stars free of charge.
Its mythy inhabitants were loose in us,
free-floating energies, nameless now.
It was April, unusually dry.
Forest fires moved through the Barrens.
We needed rain and got wind.
Once we'd have prayed, and gotten wind.
The fires reached Batsto, were stopped
in time, though our time would come.
How to live as if it would? Deeper? Wilder?
Yard sale on Clarks Landing Road.
Raffle at the church. My own yard needing
the care a good citizen would give it.
Thousands of quiet ways gradually to die.
I drove eight miles to the fire's edge.
Planes dropping water had stopped it
and a turn in the wind
and men with shovels and courage.
They didn't need to dig deep, but wide.
It was beyond them, what they had done.

5

Pascal, even your century compelled you
to feel, "We wander in times not ours."
There were authorities in those days,
there were soul-maps; it's heartening
you knew they couldn't be yours.
Here a four-wheel drive can make it through
our wilderness. The hunter-worn paths
instruct us where to turn. It seems
that much harder to get good and lost.
I dream of the rumored secret road
in Warren Grove, at the end of which
a canoe waits, and miles of winding river.
Dream, too, of the rumored Satanists there
and cats and dogs disemboweled.
I think, Pascal, you would feel
little has changed.
Cherry and apple blossoms can't distract us
long enough, or streets charged
with beautiful body, beautiful face.
Still, I can't be sure, as you were,
that what's hidden is any more mysterious
than the palpable immensity that isn't.

6

The winter winter never came—like memory
itself—moved from fact to language,
a coloration of what was seen and felt.
My ear still liked winter's doubling.
My eye was fond of its nearness to mistake.
Yet the made world had turned
to the stirrings of grass and insect,
to Oklahoma City bereft.
How little moral effort it takes to open,
then close our hearts! I found myself inclined
now to incident, now to words, conflicted,
like someone besot with spices and sauce,
wishing to stay thin.
The weather urged us out, away from worry,
that indoor work. Cut-offs and rollerblades
met us daringly at the curb, American
as pick-up trucks with rifle racks.
If we walked far enough and looked:
loosestrife, goldenrod, pixie-moss.
I knew loosestrife, I knew so many such things
before I knew their names.

7

Mornings I used to walk the dogs
by Nacote Creek, months before their deaths,
I'd see the night's debris, the tide's vagaries,
the furtive markings of creatures desperate
to eradicate every smell not theirs.
I understood those dogs, who had so little
of their own. Why not perfume
a rock, make a bush redolent
of their best selves? The boat launch
slanted waterward. The dogs avoided it,
bred for land, doomed to sniff
and cover-up and die—brothers, mine.
This was the town beach, where soon
children would vie with sandpiper and gull.
Every month, like every mind,
changed the way things looked.
I miss those mornings of the dogs.
Winter will be less wind-swept and personal
from now on, spring less observed.

8

Owned by the mayor's brother,
out of earshot of the Zoning Board's
center-of-town houses: The Shooting Place.
Farm-raised quail let loose like mice
for lazy cats, then the shotguns' heavy-metal.
Elsewhere, of course, the quail were kids
who'd gotten in the way of gangs
or their parents' close-quartered rage.
We protested anyway.
In Atlantic City, ten miles southeast,
the marshland gave way to slums
and bright lights. All nature there was human.
The six o'clock news showed the results.
Back here: pitchpine, crowberry, black oak.
Even the directions to The Shooting Place
made us want to say them. Down Chestnut Neck
to Red Wing Lake. Right at the campground.
Gone too far if you reach Beaver Run.

9

A philosopher, musing cosmically, might think
we were people who needed to be disturbed,
would say no truth ever reveals itself
to those sipping something on their porch.
I hated the cosmic as I hated a big sound
on a quiet afternoon. And I was disturbed enough,
or thought I was, for a hundred truths
to come show their wounded, open hearts.
Where were they then?
Our margaritas were rimmed with salt.
It was 5 p.m. Time even for philosophers—
sure of shelter and sufficient bread—
to take off their shoes, settle in.
Far away, men were pulling bodies from debris,
a moan the sweetest, most hopeful thing.

10

It's been their time—this winter's spring—
the shooters and the complainers
on a side not mine. They wanted America
theirs again, they said, and shouted their votes.
Mice abandoned their ingenious, fluffy homes
in attics and storage rooms, returned
to the fields. Every owl in the county knew.
Everything that couldn't think and everything
that could had made sensible plans.
At school, because it was his bold time,
a home-grown senior hot for elsewhere
asked why I stayed in South Jersey.
"Because it hasn't been invented yet," I said.
Where he saw nothing, I saw chance.
But I should have said in flat country
friends are mountains, that a place sometimes
is beautiful because of who was good to you
in the acrimonious air. So hard not to lie.
I should have said this landscape,
lush and empty and so undreamed,
is the party to which we bring our own.
I should have kept talking until I'd gotten it true.
Something about what the mouse doesn't know
and the owl does. Something intolerable
like that, with which we live.

from

RIFFS

&

RECIPROCITIES

(1998)

Poems should be more like essays and
essays should be more like poems.

—Charles Olson

Two of every sort shall thou
bring into the Ark.

—Genesis

BOURGEOIS

What we'd never let ourselves become, tra la. Especially a petit. Wasn't the edge the only place to be? Or of the working class, which would rise someday. Startling that it rose, without rancor, happily in fact, toward the bourgeoisie. Startling, too: capitalism's elasticity, that fat boy with quick feet, subtly accommodating, and not quite there when we swung. In a few long years we'd be his wary friend. We'd own mutual funds. Our property was our property, and fences were good. Parents now, we offered "Be carefuls" as often as we once cried, "Fascist pigs." Oh not petit, but grand! So what if we believed in the efficacies of art, and still spoke about our souls? So what if we still resisted the God-fearing and the Republicans and a few of their little, dispiriting rules? Each year we felt less and less dislocated at the mall. We used our remotes without irony and for entire evenings hardly moved.

RELIGION

First, it was more about mystery than about trying to get us to behave. Whichever, we're still in some lonely cave, not far from that moment a lightning storm or a sunset drove us to invent the upper reaches of the sky. Religion is proof that a good story, well-told, is a powerful thing. Proof, too, that terror makes fabulists of us all. We're pitiful, finally, and so oddly valiant. The dead god rising into ism after ism—that longing for coherence that keeps us, if not naive, historically challenged. To love Christ you must love the Buddha, to love Mohammed or Moses you must love Confucius and, say, Schopenhauer and Nietzsche as well. They were all wise and unsponsored and insufficient, some of the best of us. I'm saying this to myself: the sacred cannot be found unless you give up some old version of it. And when you do, mon semblable, mon frère, I swear there'll be an emptiness it'll take a lifetime to fill. Indulge, become capacious, give up nothing, Jack my corner grocer said. He was pushing the portobellos, but I was listening with that other, my neediest ear.

DEMOCRACY

Appalling that some people—the mendacious, the uninformed—can vote. Yet worse if they could not. Oddly, the majority does have an intelligence, sleepy-keen, animal-like, most brilliant when injured or wronged. Huey Long, for example, was loved by that animal until it knew to turn. After the votes were in, he said, "The people have spoken, the bastards." And there it was, one of democracy's successes—the loser walking away with a quip, no need for a coup. Every few years the bastards and the good guys get shuffled, redefined. Some, somehow, manage to survive the compromises and levelings of their jobs. We try to forget that capitalism itself makes more large decisions than any senator with a program or a dream. We go down to the firehouse near the creek on those Tuesdays in November. We sign in. One by one, we the imperfect have our say.

RIGHTS

What if we had the right only to sound opinions? Ah, who's to judge? say the hoi polloi. The teacher in the classroom, perhaps. The expert in the machine shop. Some lifer with a record of fairness and the severity that comes out of long caring. If we didn't make sense, we'd lose our right to another opinion for, maybe, an hour. And never could we say, "Well, that's just my opinion," or "One opinion is as good as another," without losing a few days' rights. Could more generosity be expected in the face of the shameless? If we'd said something very stupid, well then we would have to do some work in the community, say with the mentally impaired. After all, having a sound opinion is merely a minor achievement, just the beginning of good thinking. It's the least we should expect of ourselves.

SAINTS

Those who earn their names know what suffering is . . . and elect it any-
way. They love without ambivalence one shining thing, yet some—the
even more saintly—are tortured by the manifold richness of the dis-
cernible world. I've known one secular saint. I watched him fast so an
idea would swell. I didn't want to be him, though once or twice, by
design, I've felt that strange sumptuousness born from doing without.
For him it must have been an imagined feast, like a wafer on the tongue.
For me: just another something for the body to have known before it
dies and becomes dust. Saints, like revolutionaries, walk headlong into
the cool, dry wind, are always serving a hidden flame, are terrifying
because of what they do not need. The saint asks, What will you die for?
The revolutionary adds, For what would you kill? Either way, sacrifice is
an ugly business, as ugly as history itself. Choose between these terri-
ble things, history often says. We are only commentators until, for us, it
comes to that choice.

ACQUAINTANCES

Not friends. A friend, after all, is someone with whom you need not discuss important subjects, though often you do. Nor do you have to clarify the status of your relationship, except when you must. Your good news doesn't bother him too much. Bad news brings out the empathetic best in you both. And each of you knows what small misfortunes to keep to yourself. To be just an acquaintance is normal enough. But terrible to be an acquaintance when you want to be a friend. Terrible when one person is thinking *friend*, the other *acquaintance*, and, after a long separation, those rapid, uncomfortable pats on the back when they hug. Show me a back patter, and I'll show you an acquaintance lost among his intuitions, whose body's Morse code is doubt, doubt, doubt. At a party full of acquaintances, it's almost as bad. What do we say after we've said what we usually say? Better to be a stranger with small hopes and a plan.

SKY

Sky seemed the most efficient and arrogant of words, one syllable for all of that. Sky, I'd think, and would reach for an adjective. Blue or gray, if I wasn't reaching hard. Or if I'd been asleep at sunrise, or come sunset dulled by habit or drink. Sometimes, though, blue or gray was exact— the way words of uninteresting people are sometimes true, but don't seem to matter. I despised those who'd see an azure sky. I couldn't speak to anyone inclined toward cerulean. Sky. Was there ever a noun that did so much work by itself? Clouds & sun & moon were its rightful properties, & high-flying birds, & every kind of weather. But it seemed reasonable to doubt that the sky was the limit. Heaven quaintly existed in some of our minds, which remained worried by how bodies wither, disappear. Yet many times now, I'd flown above the clouds and could report only the usual magnificence. Everyone would concur—even the skeptical had seen that world—and I knew I had offered nothing and must find other attitudes, other words.

WEATHER

It had its own channel now, like rock music. But it was more like an old, fixed drama whose characters play out their tendencies, which nevertheless startles us every time. Weather's perversities were legend. Tornadoes fond of mobile homes. The excesses of rain, and those prolonged withholdings. The sky, it could be said, was the stage, the director never present, the author deeply dead for centuries. Good weather almost kept us from despair, unless we lived where the sunny days disappeared into each other and words like "self-actualized" could be heard in neighborhoods removed from migrant labor and gangs. Snow was my favorite weather, linking the treacherous and the beautiful. I trusted snow cultures above all others—shared severity bringing out good will without an irritating imperative toward fairness. It was wrong, I decided, to make plans based on forecasts. It would be like consulting an oracle long after we learned that oracles never lived anyplace but in us, knowing how mistaken we've been and how suddenly our lives— without reason—have taken a turn for the better or the worse.

FACES

High school reunions are the proving grounds Say, one's twenty-fifth. So interesting to see how character can overcome bone structure. Pretty, handsome, cute—how those attributes, those intimidations, once seemed permanent. No need to mark the many ways faces go bad. Or the sadness, for example, of remaining cute. Time is good only to those who survive its accidents, who manage to befriend it. Yet what advantages they have, the ones who start so well. They are the panthers and leopards created by an unjust god and allowed to move among the hyenas and goats. Sometimes, at any rate. We never knew how intelligence could insinuate its way into eyes and mouth, could become a kind of glamour. We never knew one could grow a face. Still, at every reunion there are a few whose beauty has deepened, sculpted by experience into a new place of consideration in our revised dreams. Barbara. Oh, I still wouldn't approach her, still wouldn't dial whatever her number had become.

BODIES

The good zoo of them, the names we could name them if we dared to begin! The muscle-bound go-away-from-me. The fleshy invite-me-in. We sit for hours in springtime and watch them pass. Only some do we undress, though we can't help but invent a life for each. We can almost tell by their walk and their arms' degree of swing how they might be in bed. We intuit those bodies we'd be impelled to obey, and bodies that would be at the mercy of ours, and bodies so kindred that all leverage would disappear. In the dark, they often curl into question marks. We love the ones that ease us beyond unease. Some, of course, are originals, seem connected to their own universe, their own first cause. Only the arrogant among us take credit for making them respond. And mine? Difficult, after a while, to love one's own—its inconsistencies, the classic diminutions, the terror of having only one. But if bodies had epitaphs, I'd want mine to read: *It rattled its cage. It wouldn't be appeased.*

LOVERS

They come to the strange city where all signs are in a language they've failed to learn. Because they're in love, however, cars stop for them when they step into danger. Waiters bring them appetizers in seven different languages, which they sample without utensils, then suck each other's fingers clean. The waiters rush home to make love to their wives. The chambermaid in their hotel has been dreaming them back, has left mints and extra towels. They can feel that strange tug. But they've learned their urgencies are sweeter the more they're delayed. It is April. They buy identical blue berets, and stroll by the river where at dusk even people who dislike each other walk arm in arm. Among them they feel disguised, though it's obvious to everyone that they come from a country that exists for only moments at a time.

FLIRTATION

In a corner at the cafe. Two of them because it takes two. All parry now, no thrust. The waiters know how to leave them alone. Outside, waiting to be seated: Illness, Boredom, Sorrow. As sure of themselves as ever. Loneliness already seated, dining with a group. For the man and woman, not much of an investment yet. Their currency disposable: hope & charm. Layers of it before the heart will be exposed. Their souls, at this stage, not in the vicinity. A tilt of the head, the puffing up, this little dance—they could be goats or birds. Too soon to be a story, just sequences. The future occurring. The eros of moving into it while keeping it at bay. The weight of survival, the daily trivia, all suspended. Between them, the unknown almost palpable now. Look, Sorrow's just been let in and given its favorite table at the far end of the room. It's taking off its cloak. They'll not see it for a while.

LUMINESCENCE

Not passion's sweaty radiance, or tantrum's righteous sheen. As far from incandescence as Garbo from Loren. Rather, a faraway kind of shining, a low temperature effect. The cold light of intelligence, sometimes. Stars and moon, of course, which inspire but don't burn. A meadow of fireflies, all those little seekers trying to find the opposite sex in the dark. The female flashes, the male flashes back. Exactly two seconds, and she'll respond again. An evening of connections. A dazzling luminescent calm. At another time, I'd favor fire's gorgeous predatory flame, shape-shifting as it moves, creating its own terms.

SERIOUSNESS

Driving the Garden State Parkway to New York, I pointed out two crows to a woman who believed crows always travel in threes. And later just one crow eating the carcass of a squirrel. "The others are nearby," she said, "hidden in trees." She was sure. Now and then she'd say "See!" and a clear dark trinity of crows would be standing on the grass. I told her she was wrong to under- or overestimate crows, and wondered out loud if three crows together made any evolutionary sense. I was almost getting serious now. Near Forked River, we saw five. "There's three," she said, "and two others with a friend in a tree." I looked to see if she was smiling. She wasn't. Or she was. "Men like you," she said, "need it written down, notarized, and signed."

SCAPEGOAT

It's the Day of Atonement, and Aaron has a brilliant idea. Two goats as offerings to the Lord. One he kills as a personal atonement for himself and his house. The other is the scapegoat. He lays both hands on its head, confessing the sins of the people, then sends it off into the wilderness. Poor goats. Lucky, unburdened people. It's easy to see why such an idea caught on. There's a burnt offering, too, involving a ram; in the face of the ineffable, Aaron tries to cover all bases. But we're most interested in the goat that bears our large and small mistakes, and carries them away from us. Leviticus knew how to tell a story, but here's what was never reported: The Lord saw the goat in the wilderness, stumbling, half dead. He said to it: A goat's life is an awful thing. This was not My intention. What they've done to you is just one more of their sins.

CRIMINAL

Born wrong. Could be as simple as that. Wrong parents. Wrong country. Or born anywhere, eminently decent, but on the wrong side of a bad law. Then there's the luck that separates forgotten incident from criminal one, like the time I accidentally set the corner lot ablaze, a nasty wind that day, no witnesses. I think, too, of the children I might have killed had they timed their carelessness just right, a trace of liquor on my breath, their ball rolling into the street, my car going slightly faster than slow. Fingerprinted. Front-paged. Instead, a normal evening at home, a citizen, nearly upright. Aren't most of us, caught or not, responsible for some kind of choice? And of course certain criminals calculate, plan, hide in the bushes, alter the books. So little separates me from them. Send us off into the wilderness without a goat, bearing our own burdens. Or maybe we deserve worse, or just to be left alone? We probably have more than one destiny, but one of them for sure is to meet up with ourselves, no Lord, no one to condemn or forgive.

from

DIFFERENT

HOURS

(2000)

SIXTY

Because in my family the heart goes first
and hardly anybody makes it out of their fifties,
I think I'll stay up late with a few bandits
of my choice and resist good advice.
I'll invent a secret scroll lost by Egyptians
and reveal its contents: the directions
to your house, recipes for forgiveness.
History says my ventricles are stone alleys,
my heart itself a city with a terrorist
holed up in the mayor's office.
I'm in the mood to punctuate
only with that maker of promises, the colon:
next, next, next, its says, God bless it.
As García Lorca may have written: some people
forget to live as if a great arsenic lobster
could fall on their heads at any moment.
My sixtieth birthday is tomorrow.
Come, play poker with me,
I want to be taken to the cleaners.
I've had it with all stingy-hearted sons of bitches.
A heart is to be spent. As for me, I'll share
my mulcher with anyone who needs to mulch.
It's time to give up the search for the invisible.
On the best of days there's little more
than the faintest intimations. The millennium,
my dear, is sure to disappoint us.
I think I'll keep on describing things
to ensure that they really happened.

NATURE

Spring's hesitant splendor had given way
to steady rains. The sky kept crumbling
and the laurels whitened and everywhere
a ripeness was visible. Nature was okay.
For me it had its place, scaffolding and
backdrop to the stage on which people
ruined and saved themselves, played out
who they were. I liked its animals best,
the big cats and the preposterous mad-God
creations like tapirs or rhinoceri.
A rose, well, a rose was
just a prom queen standing still
for a photo. Mountain sunsets,
waterfalls, they were postcards to send
to good friends who trusted happiness
occurred, if at all, in other places.
It had rained now for so many days
rain had become another form of silence.
Granted there was beauty to it as well,
gray against gray. If you stared long enough:
tiny shadings, as if someone had painted
the varieties of boredom.
And the rain made puddles on the tennis courts,
spoiling one of my pleasures.
It made some of us contemplative, soul-searching,
who had lives that couldn't bear scrutiny.
Summer was upon us. I could only hope
that it might contain enough contraries
to make it a season of plenty.
Soon I'd seek out someone not sad
to whom weather or beauty was a pretense
to get together, and drive to Cape May Point
where marshland and dune converge.

Last fall, there on the nature trail
in early morning fog, a lone man disappeared
and reappeared, in and out, until the fog
seemed to dissolve him, color him its own.
Gray, then, was the only truth in the world.

THE DEATH OF GOD

When the news filtered to the angels
they were overwhelmed by their sudden aloneness.
Long into the night they waited for instructions;
the night was quieter than any night they'd known.
I don't have a thought in my head, one angel lamented.
Others worried, Is there such a thing as an angel now?
New to questioning, dashed by the dry light
of reason, some fell into despair. Many disappeared.
A few wandered naturally toward power, were hired
by dictators who needed something like an angel
to represent them to the world.
The angels spoke the pure secular word.
They murdered sweetly and extolled the greater good.
The Dark Angel himself was simply amused.

The void grew, and was fabulously filled.
Vast stadiums and elaborate malls—
the new cathedrals—were built
where people cheered and consumed.
At the nostalgia shops angel trinkets
and plastic crucifixes lined the shelves.
The old churches were homes for the poor.

And yet before meals and at bedtime
and in the iconographies of dreams,
God took his invisible place in the kingdom of need.
Disaffected minstrels made and sang His songs.
The angels were given breath and brain.
This all went on while He was dead to the world.

The Dark Angel observed it, waiting as ever.
On these things his entire existence depended.

ODYSSEUS'S SECRET

At first he thought only of home, and Penelope.
But after a few years, like anyone on his own,
he couldn't separate what he'd chosen
from what had chosen him. Calypso,
                    the Lotus-eaters, Circe;
a man could forget where he lived.
He had a gift for getting in and out of trouble,
a prodigious, human gift. To survive Cyclops
and withstand the Sirens' song—
just those words *survive, withstand,*
                    in his mind became a music
he moved to and lived by.
How could *govern,* even *love,* compete?
They belonged to a different part of a man,
the untested part, which never had transcended dread,
or the liar part, which always spoke like a citizen.
                    The larger the man, though,
the more he needed to be reminded
he was a man. Lightning, high winds;
for every excess a punishment.
Penelope *was* dear to him,
                    full of character and fine in bed.
But by the middle years this other life
had become his life. That was Odysseus's secret,
kept even from himself. When he talked about return
he thought he meant what he said.
                    Twenty years to get home?
A man finds his shipwrecks,
tells himself the necessary stories.
Whatever gods are—our own fearful voices
or intimations from the unseen order
of things, the gods finally released him,
                    cleared the way.

Odysseus boarded that Phaeacian ship, suddenly tired
of the road's dangerous enchantments,
and sailed through storm and wild sea
as if his beloved were all that ever mattered.

AT THE RESTAURANT

*Life would be unbearable
if we made ourselves conscious of it.*
　　　　　　—FERNANDO PESSOA

Six people are too many people
and a public place the wrong place
for what you're thinking—

stop this now.

Who do you think you are?
The duck à l'orange is spectacular,
the flan the best in town.

But there among your friends
is the unspoken, as ever,
chatter and gaiety its familiar song.

And there's your chronic emptiness
spiraling upward in search of words
you'll dare not say

without irony.
You should have stayed at home.
It's part of the social contract

to seem to be where your body is,
and you've been elsewhere like this,
for Christ's sake, countless times;

behave, feign.

Certainly you believe a part of decency
is to overlook, to let pass?
Praise the Caesar salad. Praise Susan's

black dress, Paul's promotion and raise.
Inexcusable, the slaughter in this world.
Insufficient, the merely decent man.

STORY

A woman's taking her late-afternoon walk
on Chestnut where no sidewalk exists
and houses with gravel driveways
sit back among the pines. Only the house
with the vicious dog is close to the road.
An electric fence keeps him in check.
When she comes to that house, the woman
always crosses to the other side.

I'm the woman's husband. It's a problem
loving your protagonist too much.
Soon the dog is going to break through
that fence, teeth bared, and go for my wife.
She will be helpless. I'm out of town,
helpless too. Here comes the dog.
What kind of dog? A mad dog, a dog
like one of those teenagers who just loses it
on the playground, kills a teacher.

Something's going to happen that can't happen
in a good story: out of nowhere a car
comes and kills the dog. The dog flies
in the air, lands in a patch of delphiniums.
My wife is crying now. The woman who hit
the dog has gotten out of her car. She holds
both hands to her face. The woman who owns
the dog has run out of her house. Three women
crying in the street, each for different reasons.

All of this is so unlikely; it's as if
I've found myself in a country of pure fact,
miles from truth's more demanding realm.
When I listened to my wife's story on the phone

I knew I'd take it from her, tell it
every which way until it had an order
and a deceptive period at the end. That's what
I always do in the face of helplessness,
make some arrangements if I can.

Praise the odd, serendipitous world.
Nothing I'd be inclined to think of
would have stopped that dog.
Only the facts saved her.

JOHN & MARY

John & Mary had never met. They were like
two hummingbirds who also had never met.
— From a Freshman's Short Story

They were like gazelles who occupied different
grassy plains, running in opposite directions
from different lions. They were like postal clerks
in different zip codes, with different vacation time,
their bosses adamant and clock-driven.
How could they get together?
They were like two people who couldn't get together.
John was a Sufi with a love of the dervish,
Mary of course a Christian with a curfew.
They were like two dolphins in the immensity
of the Atlantic, one playful,
the other stuck in a tuna net—
two absolutely different childhoods!
There was simply no hope for them.
They would never speak in person.
When they ran across that windswept field
toward each other, they were like two freight trains,
one having left Seattle at 6:36 p.m.
at an unknown speed, the other delayed
in Topeka for repairs.
The math indicated that they'd embrace
in another world, if at all, like parallel lines.
Or merely appear kindred and close, like stars.

AFTER

Jack and Jill at home together after their fall,
the bucket spilled, her knees badly scraped,
and Jack with not even an aspirin for what's broken.
We can see the arduous evenings ahead of them.
And the need now to pay a boy to fetch the water.
Our mistake was trying to do something together,
Jill sighs. Jack says, If you'd have let go for once
you wouldn't have come tumbling after.
He's in a wheelchair, but she's still an item—
for the rest of their existence confined
to a little, rhyming story. We tell it to our children,
who laugh, already accustomed to disaster.
We'd like to teach them the secrets
of knowing how to go too far,
but Jack is banging with his soup spoon,
Jill is pulling out her hair. Out of decency
we turn away, as if it were possible to escape
the drift of our lives, the fundamental business
of making do with what's been left us.

RUBBING

Anything that you rub long enough
becomes beautiful.

—Jim Opinsky

I once saw a painter smear black paint
on a bad blue sky,
then rub it in until that lie of hers

was gone. I've seen men polish cars
so hard they've given off light.
As a child I kept a stone in my pocket,

thumb and forefinger in collusion
with water and wind,
caressing it day and night.

I've begun a few things with an eraser,
waited for friction's spark.
I've learned that sometimes severe

can lead to truer, even true.
But few things human can stand
to be rubbed for long—I know this

and can't stop. If beauty comes
it comes startled, hiding scars,
out of what barely can be endured.

THE LAST HOURS

There's some innocence left,
and these are the last hours of an empty afternoon
at the office, and there's the clock
on the wall, and my friend Frank
in the adjacent cubicle selling himself
on the phone.
                    I'm twenty-five, on the shaky
ladder up, my father's son, corporate,
clean-shaven, and I know only what I don't want,
which is almost everything I have.
                    A meeting ends.
Men in serious suits, intelligent men
who've been thinking hard about marketing snacks,
move back now to their window offices, worried
or proud. The big boss, Horace,
had called them in to approve this, reject that—
the big boss, a first-name, how's-your-family
kind of assassin, who likes me.
                    It's 1964.
The sixties haven't begun yet. Cuba is a larger name
than Vietnam. The Soviets are behind
everything that could be wrong. Where I sit
it's exactly nineteen minutes to five. My phone rings.
Horace would like me to stop in
before I leave. *Stop in*. Code words,
leisurely words, that mean *now*.
                    Would I be willing
to take on this? Would X's office, who by the way
is no longer with us, be satisfactory?
About money, will this be enough?
I smile, I say yes and yes and yes,
but—I don't know from what calm place
this comes—I'm translating

his beneficence into a lifetime, a life
of selling snacks, talking snack strategy,
thinking snack thoughts.
              On the elevator down
it's a small knot, I'd like to say, of joy.
That's how I tell it now, here in the future,
the fear long gone.
By the time I reach the subway it's grown,
it's outsized, an attitude finally come round,
and I say it quietly to myself, *I quit*,
and keep saying it, knowing I will say it, sure
of nothing else but.

THE REVERSE SIDE

The reverse side also has a reverse side.
—JAPANESE PROVERB

It's why when we speak a truth
some of us instantly feel foolish
as if a deck inside us has been shuffled
and there it is—the opposite
of what we said.

And perhaps why as we fall in love
we're already falling out of it.

It's why the terrified and the simple
latch onto one story,
just one version of the great mystery.

Image & afterimage, oh even
the open-minded yearn for a fiction
to rein things in—
the snapshot, the lie of the frame.

How do we not go crazy,
we who have found ourselves compelled
to live with the circle, the ellipsis, the word
not yet written.

ZERO HOUR

It was the hour of simply nothing,
not a single desire in my western heart,
and no ancient system
of breathing and postures,
no big idea justifying what I felt.

There was even an absence of despair.

"Anything goes," I said to myself.
All the clocks were high. Above them,
hundreds of stars flickering *if, if, if.*
Everywhere in the universe, it seemed,
some next thing was gathering itself.

I wanted to feel something,
but it was nothing more than a moment
passing into another, or was it even less
eloquent than that, purely muscular,
some meaningless twitch?

I'd let someone else make it rhyme.

AFTERLIFE

There've been times I've thought worms
   might be beneficent, speeding up,
as they do, the dissolution of the body.

I've imagined myself streamlined, all bone
   and severity,
pure mind, free to contemplate the startling

absence of any useful metaphysics, any final
   punishment or reward.
Indulgences, no doubt. Romances I've allowed myself

when nothing ached, and the long diminishment
   seemed far off.
Today I want my body to keep making its sloppy

requests. I'm out among the wayward dazzle
   of the countryside,
which is its own afterlife, wild, repeatable.

There's no lesson in it for me. I just like
   its ignorant thrust,
its sure way back, after months without desire.

Are the wildflowers holy? Are weeds?
   There's infinite hope
if both are, but perhaps not for us.

To skirt the woods, to walk deeply like this
   into the high grass,
is to invoke the phantasms of sense

and importance. I think I'm smelling the rain
   we can smell before it rains.
It's the odor of another world, I'm convinced,

and means nothing, yet here it is, and here
   sweetly it comes
from the gray sky into the small openings.

WHAT GOES ON

After the affair and the moving out,
after the destructive revivifying passion,
we watched her life quiet

into a new one, her lover more and more
on its periphery. She spent many nights
alone, happy for the narcosis

of the television. When she got cancer
she kept it to herself until she couldn't
keep it from anyone. The chemo debilitated
and saved her, and one day

her husband asked her to come back—
his wife, who after all had only fallen
in love as anyone might
who hadn't been in love in a while—

and he held her, so different now,
so thin, her hair just partially
grown back. He held her like a new woman

and what she felt
felt almost as good as love had,
and each of them called it love
because precision didn't matter anymore.

And we who'd been part of it,
often rejoicing with one
and consoling the other,

we who had seen her truly alive
and then merely alive,
what could we do but revise
our phone book, our hearts,

offer a little toast to what goes on.

THE METAPHYSICIANS OF SOUTH JERSEY

Because in large cities the famous truths
already had been plumbed and debated,
the metaphysicians of South Jersey lowered
their gaze, just tried to be themselves.
They'd gather at coffee shops in Vineland
and deserted shacks deep in the Pine Barrens.
Nothing they came up with mattered
so they were free to be eclectic, and as odd
as getting to the heart of things demanded.
They walked undisguised on the boardwalk.
At the Hamilton Mall they blended
with the bargain-hunters and the feckless.
Almost everything amazed them,
the last hour of a county fair,
blueberry fields covered with mist.
They sought the approximate weight of sadness,
its measure and coloration. But they liked
a good ball game too, well pitched, lots of zeroes
on the scoreboard. At night when they lay down,
exhausted and enthralled, their spouses knew
it was too soon to ask any hard questions.
Come breakfast, as always, the metaphysicians
would begin to list the many small things
they'd observed and thought, unable to stop talking
about this place and what a world it was.

BURYING THE CAT

Her name was Isadora and, like all cats,
she was a machine made of rubber bands
and muscle, exemplar of crouch
and pounce, genius of leisure. Seventeen years old.
A neighbor dog had broken her back,
and the owner called when he saw my car
pull into the driveway. He'd put her
in a plastic sack. It was ridiculous
how heavy she was, how inflexible.
For years I've known that to confess
is to say what one doesn't feel. I hereby
confess I was not angry with that dog,
a shepherd, who had seen something foreign
on his property. I'd like to say I was feeling
a sadness so numb that I was a machine myself,
with bad cogs and faulty wiring. But
I'm telling this three years after the fact.
Nothing is quite what it was
after we've formed a clear picture of it.
Behind our house there's a field, a half acre
of grass good for the sailing of a Frisbee.
I buried her there. My thought was to do it
before the children came home from school,
my wife from work. I got the shovel
from the shed. The ground was not without
resistance. I put several stones on top,
pyramid style, a crude mausoleum. What
we're mostly faced with are these privacies,
inconsequential to all but us. But I wasn't
thinking that then. I kicked some dirt
off the shovel, returned it to the shed.
I remember feeling that strange satisfaction

I'd often felt after yardwork, some evidence
of what I'd done visible for a change.
I remember that after their shock, their grief,
I expected to be praised.

A POSTMORTEM GUIDE

For my eulogist, in advance

Do not praise me for my exceptional serenity.
Can't you see I've turned away
from the large excitements,
and have accepted all the troubles?

Go down to the old cemetery; you'll see
there's nothing definitive to be said.
The dead once were all kinds—
boundary breakers and scalawags,
martyrs of the flesh, and so many
dumb bunnies of duty, unbearably nice.

I've been a little of each.

And, please, resist the temptation
of speaking about virtue.
The seldom-tempted are too fond
of that word, the small-
spirited, the unburdened.
Know that I've admired in others
only the fraught straining
to be good.

Adam's my man and Eve's not to blame.
He bit in; it made no sense to stop.

Still, for accuracy's sake you might say
I often stopped,
that I rarely went as far as I dreamed.

And since you know my hardships,
understand they're mere bump and setback
against history's horror.
Remind those seated, perhaps weeping,
how obscene it is
for some of us to complain.

Tell them I had second chances.
I knew joy.
I was burned by books early
and kept sidling up to the flame.

Tell them that at the end I had no need
for God, who'd become just a story
I once loved, one of many
with concealments and late-night rescues,
high sentence and pomp. The truth is

I learned to live without hope
as well as I could, almost happily,
in the despoiled and radiant now.

You who are one of them, say that I loved
my companions most of all.
In all sincerity, say that they provided
a better way to be alone.

from

LOCAL

VISITATIONS

(2003)

CIRCULAR

Daylight illuminated, but only for those
who had some knowing in their seeing,
and night fell for everyone, but harder
for some. A belief in happiness bred
despair, though despair could be assuaged
by belief, which required faith,
which made those who had it
one-eyed amid the beautiful contraries.
Love at noon that was still love at dusk
meant doubt had been subjugated
for exactly that long, and best to have music
to sweeten a sadness, underscore joy.
Those alone spoke to their dogs,
but also to plants, to the brilliant agreeableness
of air, while those together were left
to address the wall or open door of each other.
Oh for logs in the fireplace and a winter storm,
some said. Oh for scotch and a sitcom, said others.
Daylight concealed, but only for those
fond of the enormous puzzle, and night rose up
earth to sky, pagan and unknowable.
How we saw it was how it was.

KNOWLEDGE

Some things like stones yield
only their opacity,
remain inscrutably themselves.
To the trained eye they offer their age,
some small planetary news.

Which suggests the world
becomes more mysterious, not less,
the more we know.

God knows is how we begin a sentence
when we refuse to acknowledge what we know.

Gravitas is what Newton must have felt
when gravity became clear to him.

Presto, said the clown as he pulled
a quarter from behind my ear
when I was five. The very same ear in fact
that pressed itself to a snail's vacant house
and found an ocean.

The problem is how to look intelligent
with our mouths agape,
how to be delighted, not stupefied
when the caterpillar shrugs
and becomes a butterfly.

It's on a clear surface we can best see
the signs point many ways.

God knows nothing we don't know.
We gave Him every word He ever said.

SISYPHUS AND THE SUDDEN LIGHTNESS

It was as if he had wings, and the wind
behind him. Even uphill the rock
seemed to move of its own accord.

Every road felt like a shortcut.

Sisyphus, of course, was worried;
he'd come to depend on his burden,
wasn't sure who he was without it.

His hands free, he peeled an orange.
He stopped to pet a dog.
Yet he kept going forward, afraid
of the consequences of standing still.

He no longer felt inclined to smile.

It was then that Sisyphus realized
the gods must be gone, that his wings
were nothing more than a perception
of their absence,

He dared to raise his fist to the sky.
Nothing, gloriously, happened.

Then a different terror overtook him.

SISYPHUS IN THE SUBURBS

It was late and wine had wet
an aridity he'd forgotten he had.
He could feel the evening
arching above the house,
a good black dome. No ledges,
he realized, tempted him.
The once-inviting abyss
was now just a view.

Sisyphus put another CD on
and stroked the cat.
His wife was in Bermuda
with her younger sister,
celebrating the death
of winter, and a debt paid.
He missed her, and he did not.

He'd been mixing Janis Joplin
with Brahms, accountable now
to no one. The lights
from some long-desired festival
were not calling him.
No silent dog or calm ocean
made him fear the next moment.

But Sisyphus was amazed
how age sets in, how it just came
one day and stayed. And how far
away the past gets. His break
from the gods, just an episode now.

Tomorrow he'd brave the cold
sameness of the mall, look for a gift.
He'd walk through the unappeasable
crowds as if some right thing
were findable and might be bestowed.

THE UNSAID

One night they both needed different things
of a similar kind; she, solace; he, to be consoled.
So after a wine-deepened dinner
when they arrived at their house separately
in the same car, each already had been failing
the other with what seemed
an unbearable delay of what felt due.
What solace meant to her was being understood
so well you'd give it to her before she asked.
To him, consolation was a network
of agreements: say what you will
as long as you acknowledge what I mean.
In the bedroom they undressed and dressed
and got into bed. The silence was what fills
a tunnel after a locomotive passes through.
Days later the one most needy finally spoke.
"What's on TV tonight?" he said this time,
and she answered, and they were okay again.
Each, forever, would remember the failure
to give solace, the failure to be consoled.
And many, many future nights
would find them turning to their respective sides
of the bed, terribly awake and twisting up
the covers, or, just as likely, moving closer
and sleeping forgetfully the night long.

THE ARM

A doll's pink, broken-off arm
was floating in a pond
a man had come to with his dog.
The arm had no sad child nearby
to say it was hers, no parent to rescue it
with a stick or branch,

and this pleased the man to whom
absence always felt like opportunity.
He imagined a girl furious
at her younger sister, taking it out on her
one limb at a time.

Yet the sun was glancing off
the arm's little pink fingers,
and the pond's heart-shaped lily pads
seemed to accentuate an oddness,
which he thought beautiful.

When he and the dog looked for
but couldn't find the doll's body,
a different image came to him,
of a father who hated the fact
that his son liked dolls.
What was floating there

was a punishment that didn't work,
for the boy had come to love
his one-armed doll even more.
Once again the man was struck
by how much misery
the human spirit can absorb.

His dog wanted to move on,
enough of this already.
But the man was creating little waves
with his hands, and the arm, this thing
his wife was sure to question,
was slowly bobbing toward him.

BEST

Best to have a partner whose desire matches yours
so you each feel there's no time
to pull back the covers, your respective clothes
Pollocking the floor, perhaps the beautiful accident
of her bra commingling with your sock on a bedpost,
and just a stain or two to prove nothing like this
could ever be immaculate, Jesus Christ having come
involuntarily from your lips, Oh Jesus Christ,
all four of the hospital corners intact
in what has been without doubt an emergency room,
both of you having died and gone to heaven
and now, amazingly, breathing evenly once again.

CHEKHOV IN PORT REPUBLIC

No one but I took special notice of his presence,
and he hadn't come to heal, unless to render
the residual sorrow behind all our pretensions
is to heal. He was as attentive to torpor
as he was to vitality, and he knew
how pretty words and big promises could swindle,
not unlike how the church fools the poor.

Some of us had seen his black satchel, had heard
he'd helped the Jenkins woman late one night
when, bruised and bleeding, she knocked on his door.
In the old country many men beat their wives,
blaming it on vodka or weather. He didn't believe
geography made much difference; we were all the same.
And he, well he was in the business of making things

imperishable, and none of us, finally, could be saved.
He'd said the best stories require a cold eye,
his fellow humans frozen in the folly of being themselves.
But of course he tended to her wounds.
Bandages were what a doctor used. The writer
in him wanted the world made visible, exposed.

He'd taken the Olsen house set back off Chestnut.
Now and then a lady with a dog would be seen
in the driveway, though it was presumed he lived alone.
Neatly trimmed beard, eyes that seemed to forgive
even as they pierced, he resembled his photographs

before he got sick. I had no trouble believing the dead
travel between two worlds, like minds, like wind.
Something in me must have needed him here.
These would be the years (I'd see to it) his early death
deprived him of, Chekhov Chekhov once again,
the self-satisfied among us, the smug, laid bare.

POE IN MARGATE

To come back and learn his alcoholism
was an illness—Poe had to laugh at that.
He knew the vanity of excuses better than anyone,
and how good self-destruction feels when one
is in the act of it. Still, he thought, you must be sober
to write your autobiography, set things straight.

He'd give up all notions of a kingdom by the sea,
try to see things as they were and are.
But soon came the old, constant rebellion
of the senses and mind, soon he remembered
that truth was an enormous house shrouded in mist
with many secret vaults, and that perfect sobriety

is the state in which you make the version of yourself
you like best, just another way to lie. He'd have
just one drink before dinner to ease in the night,
and from his window watch monstrous Lucy the Elephant
closing up, tourists no longer walking in her body
and looking out of her eyes. The world was stranger

than he had imagined it, certainly no less strange.
The newspaper that arrived daily at his doorstep
was storied with men who murdered because voices
told them to, girls who killed their newborns
then returned to the prom. In his autobiography
he'd insist on the ultimate sanity of the artist,

regardless of what he did with his life. He'd tell
of his long hours of calculation and care,
how when Usher's house fell into that tarn
it was a victory of precision over the loose ends
of a troubled mind, how his insane narrators needed
everything that was rational in him all of the time.

HENRY JAMES IN CAPE MAY

Though the society he sought did not exist here,
no coteries of fine talk or drawing rooms
where the posturings of the privileged could be skewered,
he nevertheless took pleasure in the Victorian B&B's,
and the old, grand mansions that lined the shore.

Now in a rocker on the balcony of one of them,
the many-dormered Angel by the Sea,
he pondered the ghastliness that all immortals
were unable to die—days like this, years,
in which landscape and one's mind never changed.

Yet he'd always be the central consciousness
of wherever he was, and he trusted, inevitably,
that there'd be some Daisy or Isabel
with whom to dine, then to send out into
the common vagaries of the Cape May night.

The author as pimp, in it to plumb a discrepancy,
to watch, perhaps, one of his ladies
sit down at the wrong table, attempt to speak French
to a bunch of ruffians, say, from Rahway,
or perhaps mistake a mistress for a wife.

He'd be content to have observed for us a small
human tendency, one of the laws of the heart.
Then, for him, a Courvoisier, a good night's rest,
and a sentence that wouldn't stop, modifier
after modifier, turns, hesitations, refinements.

But was he worrying now that someone who thought
and couldn't stop thinking may never have loved?
And were we who watched him there watching us
so unfair, so spoiled, to regret that one who gave us
so much had also not given us something else?

MARY SHELLEY IN BRIGANTINE

Because the ostracized experience the world
in ways peculiar to themselves, often seeing it
clearly yet with such anger and longing
that they sometimes enlarge what they see,
she at first saw Brigantine as a paradise for gulls.
She must be a sea creature washed ashore.

How startling, though, no one knew about her past,
the scandal with Percy, the tragic early deaths,
yet sad that her Frankenstein had become
just a name, like Dracula or Satan, something
that stood for a kind of scariness, good for a laugh.
She found herself welcome everywhere.

People would tell her about Brigantine Castle,
turned into a house of horror. They thought
she'd be pleased that her monster roamed
its dark corridors, making children scream.
They lamented the day it was razed.
Thus Mary Shelley found herself accepted

by those who had no monster in them—
the most frightening people alive, she thought.
Didn't they know Frankenstein had abandoned
his creation, set him loose without guidance
or a name? Didn't they know what it feels like
to be lost, freaky, forever seeking who you are?

She was amazed now that people believed
you could shop for everything you might need.
She loved that in the dunes you could almost hide.
At the computer store she asked an expert
if there was such a thing as too much knowledge,
or going too far? He directed her to a Web site

where he thought the answers were.
Yet Mary Shelley realized that the pain she felt
all her life was gone. Could her children, dead so young,
be alive somewhere, too? She couldn't know
that only her famous mother had such a chance.
She was almost ready to praise this awful world.

MELVILLE AT BARNEGAT LIGHT

If only families could make their way
through the ether that separates
the ever-existent from the dead-and-gone,
he would have brought his family with him.
But families of the famous leave nothing
visible behind them, thus are denied
future lives. Even in death life was unfair.

Melville had known the loneliness of the sea,
months of men enduring men, the terrible
single-mindedness that comes from long nights
in your cabin with a dream. He wanted no more
of it, but here in his blue Cape Cod, two blocks
from the lighthouse, it was just himself again,
finally well-known, and no one in whom

to confide the startling emptiness of success.
Evenings he thought he could hear sounds
of life from distant and disappearing shores.
Some mornings above the steel-gray sea
the light seemed purer than ever.
Must be the lucidity, he decided, that comes when sex
no longer distracts. Must be the journey's end.

When journalists called, asking if he would permit
an interview, he'd say he preferred not to.
When asked why, he preferred not to say.
No one wanted to hear—he was sure of it—
that for every magnitude he felt an incompleteness,
for every *Moby-Dick* or *Billy Budd* he could see
thousands of words unwritten, falterings of courage.

"There goes Melville," townspeople would say, proud
that a man whose books had been made into movies
walked among them. And he, who had called for
"The sane madness of vital truth," would tip his Greek
sailor's cap and smile. On this earth, he thought,
surely there must be some vista from which all of this
would make sense, surely some final gladdening.

from

THE

INSISTENCE

OF

BEAUTY

(2004)

THE STAIRWAY

The architect wanted to build a stairway
and suspend it with silver, almost invisible
guy wires in a high-ceilinged room,
a stairway you couldn't ascend or descend
except in your dreams. But first—
because wild things are not easily seen
if what's around them is wild—
he'd make sure the house that housed it
was practical, built two-by-four by
two-by-four, slat by slat, without ornament.
The stairway would be an invitation
to anyone who felt invited by it,
and depending on your reaction he'd know
if friendship were possible.
The house he'd claim as his, but the stairway
would be designed to be ownerless,
tilted against any suggestion of a theology,
disappointing to those looking for politics.
Of course the architect knew
that over the years he'd have to build
other things the way others desired,
knew that to live in this world was to trade
a few industrious hours for one beautiful one.
Yet every night when he got home
he could imagine, as he walked in the door,
his stairway going nowhere, not for sale,
and maybe some of you to whom nothing
about it need be explained, waiting,
the wine decanted, the night about to unfold.

OPEN DOOR BLUES

The male wild turkey in the field
is all puffed up and unfurled.
Pecking at the ground, absorbed,
the female doesn't seem to care;
no sex, she seems to say,
before food. He looks the fool.
Cool air since you've been gone.
I haven't touched the heat, yet
the baseboard heaters are pinging
an atonal song. Balanced on its
haunches, your rocking chair
isn't rocking anymore. It can't,
alone, be fully what it is. I've
given it every one of its thoughts.
It thinks you'll not return.
The creature that's burrowed
inside the wall, probably a squirrel,
is chewing something with bones.
Every time I kick the spot,
it stops, but not for long.
It seems to believe it can't be hurt.
I've left the door open. The flies
know. The wasps soon will.

THE HOUSE WAS QUIET

After Stevens

The house was quiet and the world vicious,
peopled as it is with those deprived
of this or that necessity, and with weasels, too,
and brutes, who don't seem to need
a good excuse. The house was quiet as if it knew
it were being split. There was a sullenness
in its quiet. A hurt. The house was us.
It wasn't a vicious house, not yet. We hadn't
yet denuded its walls, rolled up its rugs.
It had no knowledge of the world
and thus of those who, in the name of justice,
would ransack belongings, cut throats.
Once the house had resounded with stories.
Now it was quiet, it was terrible how quiet it was.
And, sensing an advantage, the world pressed in.

DISMANTLING THE HOUSE

Rent a flatbed with a winch.
With the right leverage
anything can be hoisted, driven off.

Or the man with a Bobcat comes in,
then the hauler with his enormous truck.
A leveler or a lawyer does the rest;

experts always are willing to help.
The structure was old, rotten in spots.
Hadn't it already begun to implode?

Believe you've just sped the process up.
Photographs, toys, the things that break
your heart—let's trust

they would have been removed,
perhaps are safe with your children
who soon will have children of their own.

It's over. It's time for loss to build
its tower in the yard where you
are merely a spectator now.

Admit you'd like to find something
discarded or damaged, even gone,
and lift it back into the world.

JUAREZ

For L.

What sad freedom I have,
now that we're unwed.
I can tell the Juarez story,
which you wouldn't let me tell,
though I assured you
I'd tell it as evidence
of the strange places the soul
hides, and why I fell in love.
It was yours, you said. You
wouldn't let me make it mine.
You were in El Paso, a flight
attendant. Between jobs?
I can't quite remember. Men
gravitated to you as if they were
falling apples and you the earth.
This man you were dating, your
El Paso guy, as you called him,
said he knew a whorehouse
in Juarez, a place where
the whores danced and you could
get a table, have drinks, watch.
Let's go, he said, and you did,
with another couple,
parking your car on the U.S. side,
walking in. It was 1961.
You were adventuresome, young.
You didn't know the verb, *to slum*.
You passed an excavation site,
then some adobe shacks, children
barefoot and begging. You passed
a man on a burro. And soon
you were a turista amid the dismal
liveliness of a border town.

Your date was handsome, high-
spirited. You weren't yet sure
if he mattered to you.
The dancing whores had holes
in their underwear. One couldn't
have been more than fifteen.
They danced badly, as if bad
was what everyone wanted—
herky-jerky, lewd. Your date
was clapping. (I remember the face
you made as you said this.)
On the way back, he spoke of the fun
he'd had. Off to your right was
the excavation site.
You didn't know why,
but you climbed down into it as far
as you could go, sat curled up facing
cement blocks, the beginnings
of a foundation. Your friends thought
you a wild woman, a jokester.
But you didn't say anything.
And you wouldn't come up.
For the longest time you wouldn't
come up. Even when they went down
to get you, you wouldn't come up.
I'm sorry. If you hadn't stopped me,
I'd have been telling this
over and over for years.
By now, you'd have corrected
the errors of timing, errors of fact.
It would be that much more yours.
Or maybe you knew that a story
always belongs to its teller,

that nothing you could have said—
once it was told in my voice—
would much matter. Perhaps.
But, after all, it's my story too.
On that dark Juarez night,
every step of your troubled descent
was toward me. I was waiting
in the future for such a woman.

THE ANSWERS

After Mark Strand

Why did you leave me?

We had grown tired together. Don't you remember?
We'd grown tired together, were going through the motions.

Why did you leave me?

I don't know, really. There was comfort in that tiredness.
There was love.

Why did you leave me?

You began to correct my embellishments in public.
You wouldn't let me tell my stories.

Why did you leave me?

She is . . . I don't wish to be
any more cruel than I've been.

You son of a bitch.

Why did you leave me?

I was already gone.
I just brought my body with me.

Why did you leave me?

You found out and I found I couldn't give her up.
I was as shocked as you were.

Why didn't you lie to me?

I was already lying to you. It was hard work.
All of it suddenly felt like hard work.

Why did you leave me?

I wanted to try monogamy again.
I wanted the freedom to be monogamous.

You fucker. You fucking son of a bitch.

Why did you leave me?

I wanted you both. I thought I could be faithful
to each of you. You shouldn't have made me choose.

Don't you know what betrayal is?

I never thought of it as betrayal. More like one pleasure
of mine you should never have known.

You are really quite an awful man.

Why did you leave me?

It was time to leave.
The hour of leaving had come.

Why did you leave me?

It would take too long to explain. Please
don't ask me to explain.

Will you not explain it to me?

No, I will not explain it to you. I'll say anything
rather than explain it to you. Even things that sound true.

GRUDGES

Easy for almost anything to occur.
Even if we've scraped the sky, we can be rubble.
For years those men felt one way, acted another.

Ground zero, is it possible to get lower?
Now we had a new definition of the personal,
knew almost anything could occur.

It just takes a little training to blur
a motive, lie low while planning the terrible,
get good at acting one way, feeling another.

Yet who among us doesn't harbor
a grudge or secret? So much isn't erasable;
it follows that almost anything can occur,

like men ascending into the democracy of air
without intending to land, the useful veil
of having said one thing, meaning another.

Before you know it something's over.
Suddenly someone's missing at the table.
It's easy (I know it) for anything to occur
when men feel one way, act another.

CRUELTIES

When Peter Lorre, Casablanca's pathetic, good-hearted man,
said, "You despise me, don't you?" and Bogart replied,
"Well, if I gave you any thought, I might,"

I laughed, which the movie permitted.
It had all of us leaning Bogart's way.

"Nothing is funnier than unhappiness," Beckett has one
of his characters say, as if it might be best
to invent others to speak certain things
we've thought and kept to ourselves.

If any of us, real or fictional, had said to someone,
"Nothing's funnier than your unhappiness,"
we'd have entered another, colder realm,

like when news came that a famous writer had died
in an accident, and his rival said,
"I guess that proves God can read."
Many of us around him laughed.
Then a dark, uneasy silence set in.

All day long, my former love, I've been revising
a poem about us. First, a gentle man
spoke it, then I gave the Devil a chance.
But you always knew my someone else
could only be me.

SLEEPING WITH OTHERS

Because memory and its intrusive nostalgias
   lie down with us,
it helps to say we love each other,

each declaration a small erasure, the past
   for a while reduced to a trace,
the heart's palimpsest to a murmur.

Still, our solitudes are so populated
   that sometimes after sex
we know it's best to be quiet—

time having instructed us in the art
   of the unspoken,
or in the sufficient eloquence

of certain sighs. Regret shows up
   unpredictably,
sleeping with, but never between us.

Like joy it doesn't stay long, quickly tiring
   of the language
used in its name, wanting only itself.

We've made this bed. We're old enough
   to know sorrow may visit
now and then, and that the world slides in

at will—ugly, dark, confident it belongs.
   Nothing to do but let it
touch us, allow it to hurt, and remind.

THE ANSWERS

Won't you speak to me?

No, it would remind me
of what I haven't said.

But I need to speak to you.

I know what you need,
and your needs don't matter now.
Go talk to her about your needs.

What if I said please?

I am unreachable.
If I were standing next to you
you'd see for yourself
how far away I was.

I'll speak for you then.

Go ahead. Fine. Once again
you'll be talking to yourself.

Do you think that, maybe, over time . . . ?

There aren't enough years.

How can you be so sure?

I feel what I feel.

And is there no complicity in what you feel?
Remember, you were no saint.

There are some questions that are obscene.
There are some questions that one loses the right to ask.

I'd like to speak to you.

But I will not speak to you,
and have not spoken to you.
Admit it, and tell everyone:
Despite appearances,
I haven't said a single word.

ANOTHER DAY

Last night a succubus-bitten moon followed me all the way home,
and on the tape was a message from my friend, the mathematician,
wanting to know if I thought an apple was as elegant as a circle.
I found it impossible to muster any original response, not even
a funny one, and slept poorly, and dreamt of Brando in *Streetcar*
and, as the mind would have it, of a torturer in Pinochet's Chile,
after a hard day's work, bringing groceries home to his family.

Nothing was much better or, really, much worse, when I woke.
I wasn't thinking of possums and prairie dogs and all the sly
little things of the world peeping out of their holes, or mustangs
in Wyoming snorting in a canyon after a long run—nothing
so sweet—but of someone religious who's never had a crisis
of faith, and therefore can't be trusted. It meant I was ready to write
another version of what I'd written before, and why not? Maybe
I could ransack Schopenhauer this time. Maybe slightly alter
Augustine. Do I drift and tamper because no landscape
keeps and grounds me? Not one lascivious city. Not the most
verdant valley. I must have two souls; the empty one that aches
to be filled, and a dull, fat one. I called my friend, and said "Yes."

When it became clear I wasn't ready to do anything but drift,
it looked like another day of *if* and *I wish*, another day
in the subjunctive, and there I was, once again waiting
for something to present itself. After his car accident,
the mathematician was told he had a bruised heart
and a cracked sternum. Would he live any differently
when he got better? someone asked. "Yes," he said,
and here's why we're friends: he couldn't think
of a single way. Maybe it's the comfort of postponements
that I fear, life as rehearsal for a life. After oblivion . . . bliss,
once declared the saddest person I've ever known.

IN THE OPEN FIELD

That man in the field staring at the sky
without the excuse of a dog
or rifle—there must be a reason
why I've put him there.
Only moments ago, he didn't exist.
He might be claiming this field
as his own, centering himself in it
until confident he belongs. Or
he could be dangerous, one of those
men who doesn't know
why he talks to God.
I thought of making him a flamingo
standing alone on one pink leg,
a symbol of discordancy
between object and environment.
But I've grown so weary of inventions
that startle but don't satisfy.
I think he must have come to grieve
a good friend's death, and just wants
to stand there, numbly, quite sure
the sky he's looking at is vacant.
But I see that he may be smiling—
his friend's death was years ago—
and he might be out there to savor
the solitary elation of having discovered
what had eluded him until now.

THE WAITING

I waited for you calmly, with infinite patience.
I waited for you hungrily, just short of desperate.

When you came I knew that desperate was unattractive.
I was calm, no one wants the kind of calm I was.

It tried your patience, it made you hungry for a man
who was hungry. I am that man, I said,

but I said it calmly. My body was an ache, a silence.
It could not affirm how long it had waited for you.

It could not claw or insist or extend its hands.
It was just a stupid body, closed up and voracious.

ACHILLES IN LOVE

There was no getting to his weakness.
In public, even in summer, he wore
big boots, specially made for him,
a band of steel reinforcing each heel.
At home, when he bathed or slept,
he kept a pistol within reach, loaded.
And because to be invulnerable
is to be alone, he was alone even when
he was with you. You could sense it
in the rigidity of his carriage, as if under
his fine-fitting suits were layers of armor.
Yet everyone loved to see him in action:
While his enemies were thinking small
advantages, he only thought end game.

Then she came along, who seemed to be all
women fused into one, cheekbones and breasts
evidence that evolution doesn't care
about fairness, and a mind so good, well,
it was like his. You could see his body soften,
and days later, when finally they were naked,
she instinctively knew what to do—
as smart men do with a mastectomy's scar—
to kiss his heel before kissing
what he considered to be his power,
and with a tenderness that made him tremble.

And so Achilles began to live differently.
Both friends and enemies were astounded
by his willingness to listen, and hesitate
before responding. Even in victory he'd
walk away without angering a single god.
He wore sandals now because she liked him in sandals.
He never felt so exposed, or so open to the world.
You could see in his face something resembling terror,
but in fact it was love, for which he would die.

FIVE ROSES IN THE MORNING

March 16, 2003

On TV the showbiz of war,
so I turn it off
wishing I could turn it off,
and glance at the five white roses
in front of the mirror on the mantel,
looking like ten.
That they were purchased out of love
and are not bloody red
won't change a goddamned thing—
goddamned things, it seems, multiplying
every day. Last night
the roses numbered six, but she chose
to wear one in her hair,
and she was more beautiful
because she believed she was.
It changed the night a little.
For us, I mean.

THE INSISTENCE OF BEAUTY

The day before those silver planes
came out of the perfect blue, I was struck
by the beauty of pollution rising
from smokestacks near Newark,
gray and white ribbons of it
on their way to evanescence.

And at impact, no doubt, certain beholders
and believers from another part of the world
must have seen what appeared gorgeous—
the flames of something theirs being born.

I watched for hours—mesmerized—
that willful collision replayed,
the better man in me not yielding,
then yielding to revenge's sweet surge.

The next day there was a photograph
of dust and smoke ghosting a street,
and another of a man you couldn't be sure
was fear-frozen or dead or made of stone,

and for a while I was pleased
to admire the intensity—or was it the coldness?—
of each photographer's good eye.
For years I'd taken pride in resisting

the obvious—sunsets, snowy peaks,
a starlet's face—yet had come to realize
even those, seen just right, can have
their edgy place. And the sentimental,

beauty's sloppy cousin, that enemy,
can't it have a place, too?
Doesn't a tear deserve a close-up?
When word came of a fireman

who hid in the rubble
so his dispirited search dog
could have someone to find, I repeated it
to everyone I knew. I did this for myself,
not for community or beauty's sake,
yet soon it had a rhythm and a frame.

from

EVERYTHING

ELSE

IN THE

WORLD

(2006)

SALVATION

Finally, I gave up on obeisance,
and refused to welcome
either retribution or the tease

of sunny days. As for the can't-be-
seen, the sum-of-all-details,
the One—oh when it came

to salvation I was only sure
I needed to be spared
someone else's version of it.

The small prayers I devised
had in them the hard sounds
of *split* and *frost*.

In the beaconless dark
I wanted them to speak
as if it made sense to speak

to what isn't there.
I wanted them to startle
by how little they asked.

THE SOUL'S AGENTS

Every night before bed, say for a week,
we recommend admitting a lie
or a deception, sotto voce, a rogue's prayer
to the soul you know you have,
no matter how tattered or dormant.
Trust us, your secrets differentiate you
from no one, but the soul awakens
a little when it hears them.
We have its interests at heart,
which means your interests as well.

Try to practice unsettling
what remains settled in you—
those ideas, for example,
inherited, still untested.
And if only you could raise
your hypocrisy to the level of art,
like forgery, there might be
real hope for you.

Some people of course expect
to be rewarded for stumbling
and rising from the floor
and stumbling again, but we give
no credit for living. We favor vitality
over goodness, even over effort;
we love a great belly laugh
more than anything.

In your case we do worry
there may not be enough
quarrel in you, or enough courage
to acknowledge your worst inclinations.
Know that the soul converts them
into tenderness. Nothing pleases it more.

So next week why not admit
that what Raskolnikov did
has always made you dream?
The more you expose yourself
the more you become unrecognizable.
Remember, we are here to help.
What you decide to keep
from the world, tell us. We understand
everything. We pass it on.

MY GHOST

The desirable place is always another place,
my father said. The restlessness continues.
His voice was calm, though disembodied.
He didn't appear to be complaining.
And it doesn't matter, he added.

Even at that moment I knew I was speaking
to myself. You were dreaming, my wife said,
and I told her the half of it
that tries to masquerade as all—his exact words,
no mention of his face being mine.

It was clear from her smile
she was translating those words,
clearer still when she asked
a little too politely
if I'd please take out the dog.

But of course ours is a desirable place,
I was tempted to insist, or, How lucky,
my dear, that we're restless together.
I said neither, didn't want to feel
I had to just then. Maybe later.

An outgoing man, my father once held back
a truth that could have rescued him from sadness.
Now he roams the night, my inheritance
in every word I hear him speak. He vanishes,
returns, no place for him in this entire world.

WHAT I MIGHT SAY IF I COULD

You're a Hutu with a machete, a Serb with orders,
you're one more body in a grave they made you dig.
Or, almost worse, you're alive to tell the story,
the most silent man on earth.

Here, rhododendrons are blooming, and cicadas
are waking from their long sleep.
I need not tell you how fast a good country
can become a hateful, hated thing.

Born in the wrong place at the wrong time
to parents wronged by their parents
and ruled by some crazed utopian with a plan—
no ice-cream cone for you, no summer at the shore.

I know you can't believe suffering leads to anything
but more suffering, or that wisdom waits
in some survivor's room at the end of a hall.
What good to tell you that sometimes it does?

Sometimes has the future in it, and wisdom,
you must fear, is what victors think is theirs.
You can't even be sure of a full bowl
of rice, and you've forgotten how to sing.

Clouds with periods of sun, says our weatherman.
Unlike some of us, he never intends to lie.
Many here who look no further than their yards
believe God has a design.

WHERE HE FOUND HIMSELF

The new man unfolded a map and pointed
to a dark spot on it. "See, that's how
far away I feel all the time, right here,
among all of you," he said.
    "Yes," John the gentle mule replied,
"alienation is clearly your happiness."
But the group leader interrupted,
"Now, now, let's hear him out,
let's try to be fair." The new man felt
the familiar comfort of everyone against him.
    He went on about the stupidities
of love, life itself as one long foreclosure,
until another man said, "I was a hog,
a terrible hog, and now I'm a llama."
To which another added, "And me, I was a wolf.
Now children walk up to me, unafraid."
    The group leader asked the new man,
"What kind of animal have you been?"
"A rat that wants to remain a rat," he said,
and the group began to soften
as they remembered their own early days,
the pain before the transformation.

THE LAND OF IS

The woman whose backpack I helped lift
to the baggage rack in that suddenly sweet
compartment of a train was an art historian
from Marseilles. We talked Giotto
all the way to Naples, and fell asleep
in each other's arms.

Or was this an episode partially lived,
partially dreamed?

After my old Ford broke down in Yellowstone,
those grizzlies I invented, especially the one
standing upright near her cubs
as if declaring *no pasarán*—that story
has just the right feel.
Trust me. Even the Spanish belongs.

With that bar fight in Elko, however,
there's much still to solve. Should he be Mexican
because he was Mexican? And when,
exactly, should he pull his knife?
I keep changing my mind, sure only
of the scar on my arm—the importance
of mentioning it, I mean.

It's clear that a story not tilted
will rarely stand up. But sometimes

I find myself in the land of is, helpless
before the tyranny of this
or that sufficient thing.
That large wooden horse, for example,
with car parts for a head—the one
that silhouettes my property's edge—

I admit I placed it there, and love at dusk
to see the blackbirds ride its back
and the field of barley it overlooks
turn dark purple as night descends.

Strange horse, it is what it is,
all funk and fact, in a beautiful spot.
What could be worse?
I can't muster the slightest impulse
to make it rear up, or run amok.

REPLICAS

When it became clear aliens were working here
with their dead-giveaway, perfectly cut Armani suits,
excessive politeness, and those ray guns
disguised as cell phones tucked into their belts,
I decided we had two choices: cocktail party
to befriend them, or massive air strikes (I joked
at the Board meeting) on what might be a hospital
for children with rare diseases, but could
as easily be where these aliens spawned and lived.
Cocktail party it was, and they came
with their gorgeous women dressed like replicas
of gorgeous women, and though they sipped
their martinis as if they'd graduated
from some finishing school between their world
and ours, I must admit they were good company,
talking ball scores and GNP, even movies,
and how bright and inviting the stars seemed
from my porch. I found myself almost
having sympathy for what certain people will do
to fit in, until I remembered they might want
to take over, maybe even blow things up.
And when the dog barked from the other room,
the way she does when some creature is nearby,
about to cross an invisible line, I was sure
I couldn't afford to trust appearances ever again.
Then it was time to leave, and they left,
saying at the door what a good evening they'd had.
Each of them used the same words,
like people who've been trained in sales,
and as they moved to their Miatas and Audis
I noted the bare shoulders of their women
were the barest shoulders I'd ever seen,
as if they needed only the night as a shawl.

EVERYTHING ELSE IN THE WORLD

Too young to take pleasure
from those privileged glimpses
we're sometimes given after failure
or to see the hidden opportunity
in not getting what we want,
each day I subwayed into Manhattan

in my new, blue serge suit,
looking for work. College, I thought,
had whitened my collar, set me up,
but I'd majored in history.
What did I know about the world?

At interviews, if asked about the world,
I might have responded—citing Carlyle—
Great men make it go, I want to be one of those.
But they wanted someone entry-level,
pleased for a while to be small.

Others got the jobs;
no doubt, later in the day, the girls.
At Horn & Hardarts, for solace
at lunchtime, I'd make a sandwich emerge
from its cell of pristine glass.
It took just a nickel and a dime.

Nickels and dimes could make
a middleman disappear, easy as that,
no big deal, a life or two
destroyed, others improved.
But I wasn't afraid of capitalism.
All I wanted was a job like a book
so good I'd be finishing it
for the rest of my life.

Had my education failed me?
I felt a hankering for the sublime,
its dangerous subversions
of the daily grind.
Oh I took a dull, well-paying job.
History major? the interviewer said, I think
you might be good at designing brochures.

I was. Which filled me with desire
for almost everything else in the world.

THE UNRECORDED CONVERSATION

Isolation is the indispensable component
of human happiness.

— GLENN GOULD

Maybe genius is its own nourishment,
I wouldn't know.
Gould didn't need much more than Bach
whom he devoured
and so beautifully gave back
we forgave him his withdrawal from us.
Food frightened him, as people did,
though it was known he loved
to call Barbra Streisand at 3 a.m.
He must have liked hearing in her voice
the presence of sleep, the slightest variation.

Jeanne Moreau was in her late sixties
when I heard her say she lived alone,
adding, *by choice*—a smile in her words
missed by the interviewer who pushed
ahead, pleased to let us hear a woman
who'd learned to live *sans* men. "What
do you like best about your solitude?"
asked the interviewer. "Ah," Moreau said,
"inviting people into it," and I was Jules
or maybe Jim and in love again.

Gould retreated to his studio
at thirty-one, keeping his distance
from microphones and their germs.
He needed to control sound, edit out
imperfection. His were the only hands
that touched the keys, turned the dials.

In my dream, Moreau calls, inviting him in.
It's easy for Gould to refuse,
which he does in French,
one of his languages, and with charm,
one of the vestiges of the life
he can no longer bear to live.

SUMMER NOCTURNE

Let us love this distance, since those
who do not love each other are
not separated.
                              —SIMONE WEIL

Night without you, and the dog barking at the silence,
no doubt at what's *in* the silence,
a deer perhaps pruning the rhododendron
or that raccoon with its brilliant fingers
testing the garbage can lid by the shed.

Night I've chosen a book to help me think
about the long that's in longing, "the space across
which desire reaches." Night that finally needs music
to quiet the dog and whatever enormous animal
night itself is, appetite without limit.

Since I seem to want to be hurt a little,
it's Stan Getz and "It Never Entered My Mind,"
and to back him up Johnnie Walker Black
coming down now from the cabinet to sing
of its twelve lonely years in the dark.

Night of small revelations, night of odd comfort.
Starting to love this distance.
Starting to feel how present you are in it.

THE SLOW SURGE

How sweetly disappeared the silky distraction
of her clothes, and before that the delicacy
with which she stepped out of her shoes.

Can one ever unlearn what one knows?
In postcoital calm I was at home
in the great, minor world

of flesh, languor, and whispery talk.
Soon, I knew, the slow surge of dawn
would give way to rush hour and chores.

It would be hard to ignore the ugliness—
the already brutal century,
the cold, spireless malls—everything the mind

lets in after lovemaking has run its course,
when even a breast that excited you so
is merely companionable, a place to rest your hand.

FROM THE TOWER AT THE TOP
OF THE WINDING STAIRS

It seemed that the mountains of Vermont were hunchbacks
ringing their own silent bells, and above them
an opaque, cloudless sky a model of how to remain calm
while other parts of you might be thunder and rain.
From the tower it didn't take long to see the dangers
in believing that seeing was knowing—high flying birds
revealing our need for angels, some wispy scud
evidence of a past I'd yet to resolve. Still, wasn't
the psychological real? The tower itself had no opinion.
Men and women could be seen planting tomatoes
and rows of lettuce, touching each other goodbye,
and from this height others could be imagined creating
something wonderful out of motives like envy, even spite,
warding off, as they felt it, melancholy's encroachment.
To ascend the tower was to want not to come down.
There to the south—because I had begun to dream—
I could see congressmen suddenly released
from the prisons of their partisanship, wrestling amiably
with the imperfections of human existence. And, beyond,
enemies dropping their guns, asking for forgiveness.
Everything felt comic, how else could it be bearable?
The tower itself was proof I couldn't escape
when I escaped from the world. Out of its side window
I could see a house on fire, and in the distance
cows and goats dotting the hillside, and dogs everywhere—
no matter their size, either forlorn or frisky,
entirely dependent on the good will of others.
Soon the night birds would be calling other night birds,
the normal influx of eros begin to mix with music
heard from below. I'd feel it was time to come down,
to touch and be touched, take part in a dailiness

for which I'd need words like *welter* or *maelstrom*.
But for now if I looked hard I could see the random
pine cone, the random leaf, and if I closed my eyes
something like a pattern, the semblance of an order.

NEW

POEMS

TALK TO GOD

Thank him for your little house
on the periphery, its splendid view
of the wildflowers in summer,
and the nervous, forked prints of deer
in that same field after a snowstorm.
Thank him even for the monotony
that drives us to make and destroy
and dissect what would otherwise be
merely the lush, unnamed world.
Ease into your misgivings.
Ask him if in his weakness
he was ever responsible
for a pettiness—some weather, say,
brought in to show who's boss
when no one seemed sufficiently moved
by a sunset, or the shape of an egg.
Ask him if when he gave us desire
he had underestimated its power.
And when, if ever, did he realize
love is not inspired by obedience?
Be respectful when you confess to him
you began to redefine heaven
as you discovered certain pleasures.
And sympathize with how sad it is
that awe has been replaced
by small enthusiasms, that you're aware
things just aren't the same these days,
that you wish for him a few evenings
surrounded by the old, stunned silence.
Maybe it will be possible then
to ask, Why this sorry state of affairs?
Why—after so much hatefulness
done in his name—no list of corrections

nailed to some rectory door?
Remember to thank him for the silkworm,
apples in season, photosynthesis,
the northern lights. And be sincere.
But let it be known you're willing to suffer
only in proportion to your errors,
not one unfair moment more.
Insist on this as if it could be granted:
not one moment more.

AT THE NIHILIST'S FUNERAL

(Hope delivers the eulogy)

He was always so interestingly wrong.
I loved him, in fact for years couldn't live
without him, he who helped crystallize
what I thought by being so opposed to it.
But it's time to rejoice.
Some of the invisible roads
that run parallel to the great boulevards
can be seen now; the era of darkness-
as-illumination has passed. It was useful
while it lasted, but how nice to discover
that so few of us count on negatives
these days to preserve what we hold dear.
My friends, if you can think of me
as such, take heart. Meaninglessness
has ended its long run at the Palace.
Already, a few of us mere specks
in the universe have begun
to insist on our importance.
May the odors of lilac and laurel waft
across the river, and float over his grave
The great nihilist is dead. He'll rise again
when needed. He always has.
But those of you standing now,
having turned your backs to me in protest,
how right that you honor him so.
It's the kind of negation that he, I suspect,
would have thought might lead somewhere,
might even have thought was hopeful.

LAST WORDS

For Allen Ginsberg

I suspect that most are banalities,
and the more touching for being so,
like *Remember to feed the dog.*
Or the incoherent products of drugs
and pain, better left unrepeated.
Or something childish,
something mumbled. *Help me,*
my brother said, and continued suffering
the anonymity of the not famous.

Last words belong to the famous,
and some, like Gertrude Stein's
or Goethe's, seem rehearsed—
so witty or so plaintively profound
we recite them as we might
great lines from their work.

Ibsen's *On the contrary,*
is one of my favorites—along with
Pancho Villa's, *Don't let it end like this.*
Tell them I said something.

But what is it about Ginsberg's
I'm tired and I have to go to sleep
that moves me so? Is it the suggestion
of completion, of nothing left untasted,
risks taken, a life fully lived?
His great incantatory howl behind him,
he slipped into history
with a declarative sentence,
he who had unmuzzled a generation,
jazzed it, sent it careening forward.

THE PERFECT LIFE

Because it was in the future, it always existed
and asked of us, I thought, only to wish
ourselves toward it, and record what we saw,
its flora and architecture and scud-free sky.
And I, for one, found this to be possible,
and wished myself further into it,
so far that I heard it asking me to tell others
about the evils of industry,
and how it might feel to have our desires
matched, then satisfied, every day of our lives.

The perfect life was never quite present,
so could never be faulted, and seemed
to keep just enough of its promises
to keep me committed. In this way it resembled
one of those beautiful strangers
made of smoke and thin air, the lovely trouble
I've often foreseen, but still wanted to lie down with.

I remember how often I forgave its intolerances,
and once, when I realized its agenda was to exclude
every other version of a perfect life, I excused it
as fulfillment's necessary sacrifice.
Later on—oh the perfect life doesn't like the sound
of history—later on, amid the regret, the heartbreak—
amid such words I now permitted myself to say,

I nevertheless remember a clearing by a river,
the camaraderie there, the small fires and the dancing,
and looking up into the lambency of the night
how I believed that all of it was ours.

AREN'T THEY BEAUTIFUL?

Aren't they beautiful,
she said, with an edge,
because I hadn't commented
on these slender,
some would say splendid
purple things
we'd come upon. The foxglove,
she repeated, aren't they beautiful?

Foxglove, what a nice name,
I thought, I liked that name,
and told her so, but I was thinking
of conversation, the way *beautiful*
often puts an end to it.
And remembered as a child
those long drives in the country—
Look! a clearing. Look!
a swatch of wildflowers.

All the tedium of ahs and yeses,
all that piety before the perfect.

Beauty, for her, was a beginning,
an honest way in. I knew that,
yet still I wanted to say, Give me
what a troubled soul might see,
give me *that* kind of beautiful,
but heard the sanctimony in it,

told the truth instead, the truth
that also digs one's grave,
becomes its own epitaph.
Until you asked, I said,
I saw nothing, almost nothing.

Deprivation is the mother of beauty,
a wittier man might have declared,
pointing theatrically
to all this blinding abundance.
Or simply admitted he was a prisoner
of his prejudices, helplessly himself.

The foxglove were looking smug,
uncontestable. And there I was,
impatient, angling for an argument.
We were standing directly in front
of those tall, pendulous eye-catchers.
What do you see now? she asked,
you're staring right at them.

The lies of daylight, the failures of language,
God the vicious, hiding behind another veil.

LANGUAGE: A LOVE POEM

After Neruda

When I say your hair
is the color of a moonless night
in which I've often been lost,
I mean approximately that dark.
And the dove outside our window
is no symbol, merely wakes us
at dawn, its mate a grayish creature
that coos quite poorly. Peace
is an entirely different bird.
The rose, to me, signifies the rose,
and the guitar signifies
a musical instrument
called the guitar. At other times
language is a slaughterhouse,
a hammering down, its subjects hanging
from hooks, on the verge
of being delicious. When I say
these things to you it's to watch
how certain words play
themselves out on your face,
as if no one with imagination
can ever escape being a witness.
The whale, for example, no matter
its whiteness, is just a mammal
posing as a big fish, except
of course if someone is driven
to pursue it. That changes everything.
Which is not to suggest I don't love
the depth of your concealments.
When I say your name over and over
it's because I cannot possess you.

PLEASE UNDERSTAND

(A Bachelor's Valentine)

When, next day, I found one of your earrings,
slightly chipped, on the steps leading up to
but also away from my house,

I couldn't decide if I should return it to you
or keep it for myself in this copper box.
Then I remembered there's always another choice

and pushed it with my foot into the begonias.
If you're the kind who desires fragile mementos
of these perilous journeys we take,

that's where you'll find it. But don't knock
on my door. I'll probably be sucking the pit
out of an apricot, or speaking long distance

to myself. Best we can hope for on days like this
is that the thunder and dark clouds will veer elsewhere,
and the unsolicited sun will break through

just before it sets, a beautiful dullness to it.
Please understand. I've never been able to tell
what's worth more—what I want or what I have.

HISTORY

It's like this, the king marries
a commoner, and the populace cheers.
She doesn't even know how to curtsy,
but he loves her manners in bed.
Why doesn't he do what his father did,
the king's mother wonders—
those peasant girls brought in
through that secret entrance, that's how
a kingdom works best. But marriage!
The king's mother won't come out
of her room, and a strange democracy
radiates throughout the land,
which causes widespread dreaming,
a general hopefulness. This is,
of course, how people get hurt,
how history gets its ziggy shape.
The king locks his wife in the tower
because she's begun to ride
her horse far into the woods.
How unqueenly to come back
to the castle like that,
so sweaty and flushed. The only answer,
his mother decides, is stricter rules—
no whispering in the corridors,
no gaiety in the fields.
The king announces his wife is very tired
and has decided to lie down,
and issues an edict that all things yours
are once again his.
This is the kind of law
history loves, that contains
its own demise. The villagers conspire
for years, waiting for the right time,

which never arrives. There's only
that one person, not exactly brave,
but too unhappy to be reasonable,
who crosses the moat, scales the walls.

THE MERMAID

My comb made of white coral
was missing, the next day
my sea-weed braided belt.
I of course knew the old stories
they believe. Truth is, I always let
them take something of mine;
they feel in control,
they come to me like gods.
For this one in particular I was
a feast. No, I was abundance
and that other thing
that never fails to fascinate—
I let him believe it moved that way
only because of him.
It ruins them eventually, what they
can never have again.
But I seem to need more than one
kind of familiar thing. Tentacle,
hand—so many worlds
of pleasure beckon and call.
And how my breasts love
the dolphin's nose, the human mouth.
I know where he's hidden
my belt and comb, and soon

I'll reach for that ledge
of our cave and pull them down.
In time he'll settle for someone
he believes keepable,
but more women than he realizes
have needs like mine.
Oh, an explanation rarely does
anyone any good,
though I know he'll ask for one,
and the many-voiced sea—
whose edge he'll have come to—
will whisper words
he'll choose to hear his own way.
Meanwhile, the water is a constant
caress, and my hair attracts
the sleekest, most curious of fish.
Soon—I wish I could tell him—
I'll also tire of this.

THE ROOM

The room has no choice.
Everything that's spoken in it
it absorbs. And it must put up with

the bad flirt, the overly perfumed,
the many murderers of mood—
with whomever chooses to walk in.

If there's a crowd, one person
is certain to be concealing a sadness,
another will have abandoned a dream,

at least one will be a special agent
for his own cause. And always
there's a functionary,

somberly listing what he does.
The room plays no favorites.
Like its windows, it does nothing

but accommodate shades
of light and dark. After everyone leaves
(its entrance, of course, is an exit),

the room will need to be imagined
by someone, perhaps some me
walking away now, who comes alive

when most removed. He'll know
from experience how deceptive
silence can be. This is when the walls

start to breathe as if reclaiming the air,
when the withheld spills forth,
when even the chairs start to talk.

❧

WORRY

My friends, the worriers, make themselves miserable,
I suppose, in preparation for the misery to come.
They must be practicing for the time lightning will destroy
their houses, or for when their spouses will die
on that famous fog-plagued strip of road. Bird flu
and if their hotel room will be too close to the ice machine
often begin to live side by side in their minds.
They can't help it, they say, these savants of catastrophe.
I'd rather be like you, they say, but can't,
often adding that I seem to suffer from underworry,
which causes them to worry for and about me the more.
And so, since worry always trumps the absence of worry,
to live with them is to live on their terms. Don't worry,
I've learned not to say, which is other-planetary language
to them, cold, unsympathetic, the language of someone
who wouldn't help them build a bomb shelter
after they'd seen the end of the world in a dream.
Try to be reasonable, is the button that triggers the bomb.
I try to love them for their other qualities,
like being right about most other things, or how good
they are in the kitchen or the workplace or the bed.
But if not for my sake, then for their own, shouldn't
they worry less, or at least privately? Every once in a while
shouldn't they say, Forgive me my worries?
But a semi is always running a stop sign, one of the big
hemlocks topples in a storm. Then they point to the world.
What's wrong with me, they want to know.
Don't I know what's out there? A failure of imagination,
they say. A man who's a clear danger to himself.

THE BOOK AND I

Already I lived in an unmanaged world—
from a book I needed something different.
And along the way it wouldn't hurt,
I kept thinking, if I could please, please,
be enthralled. I put it down—
the merciful language you use
when you've decided the poor dog
would be better off dead. I put the book down
and began to clip the coleus. I made
some long-overdue calls to my relatives,
old attempts at reining in the chaos.
The book remained on the coffee table,
its characters as good as gone, the plod
of their progress now forever curtailed.
They had been sad characters, but in a book
I wanted sadness tuned so it might
give pleasure, I wanted it oddly funny,
or to brilliantly unsettle my heart.
These characters were only sad,
the father cruel but undriven
by any flaws I might share, the son—
like the author—unreliably unreliable.
Some books fail so maddeningly
I've tossed them across the room,
which means they'd been loved
until they broke some big promise,
or forgot one was made.
This book I just wanted to go
quietly, perhaps to some yard sale.
There'd be no afterlife for it, no,
no place for it even on the highest,
out-of-sight shelf in the house.
After all, the others were up there,
my chosens, all spine and substance.

MERCY

The music was fidgety, arch,
an orchestral version of a twang.
Welcome to atonal hell,
welcome to the execution
of a theory, I kept thinking,
thinking, thinking. I hadn't felt
a thing. Was it old fashioned
of me to want to? Or were feelings,
as usual, part of the problem?
The conductor seemed to flail
more than lead, his baton evidence
of something unresolved,
perhaps recent trouble at home.
And though I liked the cellist—
especially the way
she held her instrument—
unless you had a taste
for unhappiness
you didn't want to look
at the first violinist's face.
My wife whispered to me,
This music is better than it sounds.
I reminded myself the world outside
might be a worse place
than where I was now,
though that seemed little reason
to take heart. Instead
I closed my eyes, thought about
a certain mezzo soprano
who could gladden a sad day
anywhere, but one January night
in Milan went a full octave
into the beyond. Sometimes escape

can be an art, or a selfishness,
or just a gift you need
to give yourself. Whichever,
I disappeared for a while,
left my body behind to sit there, nod,
applaud at the appropriate time.

ABANDON

Chelsea, 2006

All afternoon, witnessing loopy splashes of color
in one gallery, what seemed like someone's
hieroglyphics to himself in another,
the huge often in cahoots with the minimal,
and everywhere a terrible strain to be different,

I understood why men like me tend not to go
to gatherings where people display their psyches
and show off their piercings. In short, I felt like
a conservative, and a smug one at that.
I began to long for still lifes, shadow-filled,

apples and pears bruised just right by someone
who also liked geometry, or for some dark
and brutal Caravaggio, or one of those Hoppers
where a woman, apparently stunned
by the night before, is staring out a window.

Outside, dusk was vying with sunlight,
the gray buildings on 9th Avenue yielding
every second to a different shade of gray. Lovely,
I thought, then found myself wishing
for some swirl of Matisse-like gaiety.

Oh, it was clear I needed to abandon the self
I'd brought with me, that inveterate spoilsport,
the way an early surrealist must have abandoned
the well-trained good boy in himself
to enjoy the desecration of a rose.

An old feeling: What a good time I might be having
if only I could have left myself home.
But there I was, walking to the subway,
artless, empty-handed, still largely in love
with my prejudices. The beggar at the foot

of the stairs looked like a detail from a Brueghel.
I gave him some change, and made my way down
to the Uptown side where many years before—
when I lived to be surprised—I'd watched a man
with a guitar sing while his monkey danced.

AN ABBREVIATED TOUR
OF THE NOT YET FALLEN WORLD

The light would shine
then the night would fall,
and in those bedroom towns
outside cities
where many had gone
to escape the poor,
people I'd once been
and sometimes still am—
with investments and neuroses
and best intentions postponed—
would sleep a guarded sleep,
alert to the slightest sound.

The children would wake to daylight
they tended to ignore,
and all over our houses
screens would flicker
with new privacies, each to his own.
At work, I, too, rarely moved,
waiting at my machine
for the sudden to occur.
Even my disconnections
had a pleasing speed.

And when I wanted to move,
to literally fly,
the sky was forbidden
if I couldn't prove
I was my name.
Or, my license out, shoes off,

almost in the clear,
an agent might hold up
nail clippers, toothpaste,
want to know my secret plans.

I might then be asked to spread
my legs, extend my arms,
as if humiliation were a passage
to another world, and I'd be off
to some Houston or Atlanta,
a place they'd want me to agree
was my final destination.

Home would feel different
any time I'd reason to believe
I might not safely return.
Once, after circling in turbulence
then skidding on the runway,
living room took on new meaning.
I put my feet up on the ottoman,
and with a glass of Glenlivet
luxuriated in the company
of everything taken for granted.
Night wasn't falling, I could see it
slipping in through the trees,
rising from the marshes.
Nothing in it, I was sure,
contained a message.

Next morning, like every morning,
the dog moaned
about the same time sunlight
found a crack in the curtains.
No need for an alarm.
Juice and pastry and pills,
the newspaper open
first to yesterday's box scores
before any details
of our collective disgraces—

oh, how easy it is to control
how things begin.

I even saved the funnies for last,
as if such an order, because it was mine,
could possibly matter.

THE SEASON OF GRANDEUR AND LIES

I've had no more deathly thoughts in fall
than in any other season, and doubt
that dark encroachment some claim to feel
as they watch leaves turn and trees yield
to reveal their austere, skeletal beauty.
Maybe Keats did, but that's because
he was actually dying, every day coughing up
phlegm, which, for all we know, may have
reminded him of autumn's colors.
Great poets, though, aren't committed
to whatever just dawns on them or appears.
"To Autumn" is so good it makes me want
to stay alive. If ever he considered *phlegm*
to describe, say, a rain-soaked golden leaf,
his better self must have vetoed it,
knew what to allow in, what to suppress.
After all, he had "mellow fruitfulness"
to live up to, all that language rich and right.
It's so easy to falsify what one sees,
then how one feels. Those poets who would
have us thinking of our fathers as we walk
among apples recently fallen and bruised—
they don't mean to lie. They just slide too far
into the seductions of saying this is like that.
If I found myself among apples scattered
on the ground, I'd likely wonder who didn't
pick them, and why. Yet even if death were
to cross my mind, I think I'd just let it cross.
What's ripe so often lingers before it falls.
I prefer to be taken by surprise.

EXCITEMENT

For years I sought it, had it,
the physical kind—visceral
and a little dangerous—
and would try to wear it
like a bright shirt
so that others might recognize
and be drawn to it,
perhaps want,
with my assistance,
to investigate it further.

But I've watched with curiosity
that kind of excitement
slowly give up its spot
at the top of my day,
in effect watched it
learn to play with others,
like its faraway cousin,
Contemplation,
like its little-known peer,
Emotional Generosity.

Excitement, I might think
to myself on days like today,
and mean something quiet
or tender, or, yes,
passionately quiet and tender,
or maybe even selfish,
and be reminded
that to redefine is not always
to lose. Astonishing

that sometimes we don't
quite have to kiss
what we've loved goodbye.

AND SO

And so you call your best friend
who's away, just to hear his voice,
but forget his recording concludes
with "Have a nice day."

"Thank you, but I have other plans,"
you're always tempted to respond,
as an old lady once did, the clerk
in the liquor store unable to laugh.

Always tempted, what a sad
combination of words. And so
you take a walk into the neighborhood,
where the rhododendrons are out
and also some yellowy things

and the lilacs remind you of a song
by Nina Simone. "Where's my love?"
is its refrain. Up near Gravel Hill
two fidgety deer cross the road,
whitetails, exactly where

the week before a red fox
made a more confident dash.
Now and then the world rewards,
and so you make your way back

past the careful lawns, the drowsy backyards,
knowing the soul on its own
is helpless, asleep in the hollows
of its rigging, waiting to be stirred.

.

THE MISTAKEN

When a sparrow or grackle mistakes my window
for clear passage, often its neck is broken—
no chance for it to ever get smarter.
And the hawk pursuing it has less than a second
to understand that sometimes the world isn't
what it seems; surely not enough time for wisdom.
Which is why I'm most pleased when they're stunned
and lie there for a while, then rise unsteadily,
stand dazed a while longer. They could be us,
or at least those of us with a tendency to mistake
the unforgiving cinderblock of one of our bad ideas
for a pillow. How lovely, though, when they become
themselves again and take to the trees,
as if eager to tell others what they've learned.
For birds salvation isn't very complicated—
a good meal or two, a few life or death maneuvers
in hostile skies. And how lovely that they don't
need an invisible Bird-of-all-birds to bring
twigs and worms to, that they aren't supplicants
before their own creation.
That error seems to be exclusively ours.
Tomorrow, though, once again the sparrow
will be fooled by the lure of the transparent.
The only history the hawk will remember
will have something to do with what's irresistible
and delicious. And the timid among us
will continue to politely nod while the powerful
sanctify what they feel like doing, and I for one
won't be able to deny I haven't so nodded.
Cruelty? Only wild things need no excuses.
Yet what good are ours? We often say
we were blinded. We say we were not ourselves.

WHAT MEN WANT

Among the powerless,
unable to stop the ache that came
after someone else got the job
or the raise, my father just wanted
a little respect, some affirmation,
not always to be ruled
by the clock. My brother, too,

good man unequipped
to seize a day or leave a job
where everyone yelled,
brought the yelling home
the way others bring bread.
How else to make
his presence felt? And I,

in my chosen, happy torment
of words, spend entire days
cutting, stitching, rearranging,
trying to do what it takes
to be properly heard. Other days
I speak about books I love.
I feel like an escapee,
one big step ahead of my past.

Now I can afford to buy a ticket
to someplace else.
Now I can choose not to go.
Sometimes a man wants
because he discovers he can have.

No doubt this is why there are laws,
and why I'm grateful to my father
when I go too far
and covet, say, that Maserati
with its nifty slide-back roof
and five-on-the-floor.
My father who knew too well
what happiness isn't—his voice
inside me declaiming its clear No.

I wear his silver watchband,
a keepsake, for the sake of keeping.

What a man wants is to be rescued
from what he's not,
to test, then see what remains
of his inheritance.

And I'd like to think our hearts
are also in the business
of discovering their size,
and that another way to revise
is by adding on.

On weekends, my brother
would retreat to his garage,
desiring some honest praise
for fixing something broken.
Sometimes he'd want an evening out
with the boys, the indulgence
of shouting at an umpire,
or some merciless taking to task
of a slumping player.

After his stroke shocked
and rewired him, his anger left;
he never yelled again. Funny man
until the end, insistent hand holder,
at sixty-one he discovered
tenderness, witnessed the giving of it
come back to him.

No amount of justice or love
could have saved him, of course,
though just a little for a little while
must have felt like everything.

I want my list of everything
to include the approximate location
of the abyss, and its tolerance
for flirtation. I want no one
at the high stakes table
to intuit my pocket aces,
no one, any place, to suspect
that what I choose to reveal
is my way of withholding.

What a man wants is the power
to name the terms of his rescue,

and to know when it's time
to close the curtains,
usher in the private,
no longer live or resist
anyone else's story.

My father was a salesman
who meant every word he said,
though sometimes in a room
of strangers he'd shake
someone's hand too long,
or his smile would look
like a stuck, decided-on thing.

Just be yourself, he once counseled.
Who would want to know me then,
I thought, who would forgive me?

I've always needed paper and pencil
in order to speak as little as I should.
After the power to choose
a man wants the power to erase.

ACKNOWLEDGMENTS

The selected poems in this volume have appeared in the
following books, all published by W. W. Norton & Company.

Loosestrife (1996)
Riffs & Reciprocities (1998)
Different Hours (2000)
Local Visitations (2003)
The Insistence of Beauty (2004)
Everything Else in the World (2006)

The new poems have appeared in the following journals:

Agni: "Please Understand"
American Literary Review: "The Season of Grandeur and Lies"
American Poetry Review: "Aren't They Beautiful," "And So,"
    "The Book and I," "The Mermaid," "Worry"
Alaska Review: "Excitement"
The Georgia Review: "Talk to God," "Language: A Love Poem,"
    "An Abbreviated Tour of the Not Yet Fallen World"
New Ohio Review: "Mercy"
The New Yorker: " The Room," "History"
The Paris Review: "At The Nihilist's Funeral"
Prairie Schooner: "What Men Want," "The Perfect Life,"
    "The Mistaken"
The Tiferet Journal: "Last Words"

"Open Door Blues" was selected for *The Best American Poetry* 2003
    (Scribner)
"Five Roses in the Morning" was selected for *The Best American
    Poetry* 2005 (Scribner)
"The Land of Is" was selected for *The Best American Poetry* 2006
    (Scribner)
"Where He Found Himself" was selected for *The Best American*

Poetry 2007 (Scribner)

"Salvation" won a Pushcart Prize in 2006

Loosestrife was a finalist for The National Book Critics Circle Award
   (1996)

Different Hours was awarded the Pulitzer Prize (2001)

Everything Else in the World was a finalist for The Paterson Prize for
   Sustained Literary Achievement (2006)

My thanks to Lawrence Raab for his steadfast and invaluable attention
to almost all of these poems over many years. And to Jill Rosser for her
scrupulous readings. And to Barbara Hurd for the everything she's given
me, and to the love that sustains.

A special thanks to Carol Houck Smith, friend, and editor of all these
books. What luck to have found you!

INDEX OF POEM TITLES AND FIRST LINES